Sport Officiating

Sport officials are tasked with maintaining order and adjudicating sport contests. Given their multifaceted role in enforcing rules, standardizing competitions, and keeping sport safe for all participants, they are a requisite part of the sport workforce.

With ongoing reports of annual attrition rates in officiating in excess of 20–35% for various sports around the world, there is more than ample evidence that officiating dropout is a persistent, pervasive, and global challenge underpinned by multiple contributing factors including, but not limited to, the threat of verbal and physical abuse. Moreover, despite worldwide recognition and growing interest in the problem, there has not been a comprehensive resource for sport scientists and practitioners studying or working to reverse the ongoing trend.

Sport Officiating: Recruitment, Development, and Retention provides a 'state of the science' summary in the emerging area of inquiry limited to sport officiating recruitment, development, and retention, and provides insight and evidence-based approaches to the development of successful officiating development programs (ODP).

This book is a primary reference work using a multifaceted, holistic, and evidence-based approach to integrate key findings from the sport science literature to date in suggesting and providing real-world solutions to the practical issues faced by sport organizers.

Sport Officiating: Recruitment, Development, and Retention is a key resource for researchers interested in the development of sport officials and for sport practitioners aiming to implement officiating development programs (ODP) at any level within sport systems.

Lori Livingston is the Provost and Vice-President, Academic and a Professor in the Faculty of Health Sciences at Ontario Tech University in Oshawa, Ontario, Canada.

Susan L. Forbes is an Adjunct Professor and Manager of the Teaching and Learning Centre at Ontario Tech University in Oshawa, Ontario, Canada.

Nick Wattie is an Assistant Professor in the Faculty of Health Sciences at Ontario Tech University in Oshawa, Ontario, Canada.

Ian Cunningham is a Research Associate in the Faculty of Health Sciences at Ontario Tech University in Oshawa, Ontario, Canada.

Routledge Research in Sport Business and Management

For more information about this series, please visit https://www.routledge.com/Routledge-Research-in-Sport-Business-and-Management/book-series/RRSBM

Sport Officiating
Recruitment, Development, and Retention

Lori Livingston, Susan L. Forbes,
Nick Wattie, and Ian Cunningham

Routledge
Taylor & Francis Group

LONDON AND NEW YORK

First published 2020 by Routledge

2 Park Square, Milton Park, Abingdon, Oxon OX14 4RN
605 Third Avenue, New York, NY 10017

Routledge is an imprint of the Taylor & Francis Group, an informa business

First issued in paperback 2022

Publisher's Note

The publisher has gone to great lengths to ensure the quality of this reprint but
points out that some imperfections in the original copies may be apparent.

Library of Congress Cataloging-in-Publication Data
Names: Livingston, Lori, 1959– author.
Title: Sport officiating : recruitment, development, and
retention / Lori Livingston, Susan L Forbes, Nick Wattie and
Ian Cunningham.
Description: New York, NY : Routledge, 2020. | Includes
bibliographical references and index.
Identifiers: LCCN 2019059000 (print) | LCCN 2019059001
(ebook)
Subjects: LCSH: Sports officials—Recruitment. | Sports
officials—Training of. | Sports officiating.
Classification: LCC GV735 .L58 2020 (print) | LCC GV735
(ebook) | DDC 796—dc23
LC record available at https://lccn.loc.gov/2019059000
LC ebook record available at https://lccn.loc.gov/2019059001

ISBN: 978-1-138-61057-6 (hbk)
ISBN: 978-1-03-233641-1 (pbk)
DOI: 10.4324/9780429465291

Typeset in Sabon
by codeMantra

To the greatest role models an aspiring official could have – Donna Misener, Jenny Kyle, Lanetta Ware, and Marge Garinger – thank you for your guidance, mentorship, and professionalism. – LAL

We have a responsibility to live up to the legacy of those who came before us by doing all that we can to help those who come after us (a quote from Michele Obama). – SLF

To Julia and Samuel, always. – NW

To my pillar Gillian, sport ambassador Coach James Carl, and character builder Amanda. – IJC

Contents

Figures

Tables

Preface

This book is written from the heart. It is the product of many years of involvement in sport – by all four authors – as athletes, coaches, consultants, administrators, researchers, and officials. We know sport, live sport, and love sport on a daily basis. And we consider ourselves fortunate, albeit in a rather serendipitous fashion, to have come together as a collective at Ontario Tech University to put our thoughts on paper.

My exploration into sport officiating as an area of research interest began almost 20 years ago. At that point in time, I had just decided to step down after spending 15 years as a nationally ranked umpire in the sport of women's field lacrosse. I had officiated games involving athletes as young as the age of six years up to and including junior and senior national team athletes, varsity athletes at the high school and university levels, and the occasional international test match. I had travelled across Canada and around the world as part of the sport of women's lacrosse, and my affinity to the sport and my role as an official was iron clad. The decision to discontinue officiating was anything but easy to make. That is when I read a story published online by the Canadian Broadcasting Corporation (CBC) extolling that officials were leaving sport at an alarming rate because of the verbal abuse they were experiencing.

I found myself at odds with the news story because that was not my story. I had certainly been on the receiving end of many verbal challenges from players, coaches, and spectators over the years – but they were the least of my reasons for stepping away from umpiring. In fact, my departure was linked to considerably different circumstances, that is a major knee injury coupled with moving for career purposes to a province where the sport of women's field lacrosse was not played. I felt strongly that there needed a more fulsome review of the question as to why sport officials were choosing to leave the role and that these alternate stories needed to be told. Along with my colleague, Dr. Susan L. Forbes, we began a research journey into the topic of sport officiating. We started asking the question as to why sport officials were leaving the role, but by 2010 we came to realize that many others were starting to or had explored the same issue. That is when we decided to flip the question to explore why officials were opting into the role and choosing to stay.

The question of why officials stay is exceptionally important and it is the question that provides the basis for this book.

The journey to get this book into print has been both rewarding and frustrating. Sport officials are often marginalized and devalued within the world of sport, and the body of scientific literature dedicated to them has historically been underdeveloped. The good news is that this is changing as they are now gaining more attention from sport scientists and the role of sport officials seems to be increasingly valued within sport itself. We have done our best to weave evidence-based research into the content of this book in a very practical way that also highlights the incredible complexity of 'officiating', and the works of Drs. Wattie and Cunningham have added depth and new perspectives to the discussion. The information is important, but so too is the ability of the reader to translate it into meaningful everyday actions and practices within sport organizations. To this end, the reader will find useful tips and take-home messages in each chapter.

In closing, I would like to thank all of the sport organizations that have supported our efforts over time. You know who you are – there are many of you – and we are very grateful. Ultimately, this book is dedicated to every past, present, and future sport official. Thanks for making a difference through your contributions. You are irreplaceable within the world of sport.

Lori A. Livingston, PhD
Oshawa, Ontario

Acknowledgments

This work was supported by funding from the Social Sciences and Humanities Research Council (SSHRC) of Canada and a Sport Participation Research Initiative Grant (Grant# 435-2018-1496). We would also like to acknowledge and thank Ontario Tech University MHSc student Jason Mergler, whose thesis research helped inform many of the ideas within this book. Finally, we extend thanks and appreciation for the incredible support provided by Sport Canada, Ontario Soccer, Ontario Basketball, and numerous other amateur sport organizations and officials in Canada who shared their stories with us and inspired this book.

1 Introduction to Recruiting, Developing, and Retaining Sport Officials

Bailey Slusher is an ordinary teenager. He lives in Indiana, has graduated from high school, and is now completing college-level business administration courses. He is also an avid sports fan and has grown up in a sport-loving family. His brother Brevin plays high school varsity basketball and his father Neil is a former basketball coach. Bailey, in contrast, is a basketball referee. In the April 2018 issue of *Referee* magazine, Bailey is described as having an "intense love" for basketball officiating (Windler, 2018, p. 65). For those that pursue officiating, many do so because of their love for the sport (Livingston et al., 2017). Hence, Bailey's reason for officiating, relative to others that engage in the avocation, is not unique. The Slusher family, moreover, provides a common portrait of organized sport involvement in North America. They are illustrative of the tendency for multiple members of a given family, including individuals from different generations, to be involved in the same sport in either similar or differing roles. And there are many such roles to choose from, including those that provide support for (e.g., administrators, team managers, spectators, and others) versus those that require direct participation within competition (i.e., athletes, coaches, and officials). In terms of the latter grouping, Brevin as an athlete represents the largest participant cluster, while coaches, like dad Neil, represent the second largest member group. As an official, Bailey represents the smallest – and dare we say most important yet least celebrated or appreciated – cohort of direct sport participants. This may seem like a rather bold statement; however, without rules (and therefore officials), sport is merely reduced to play. To understand this perspective, one needs to view sport as being more than a game or leisure activity.

Sports represent games or competitions of physical prowess which have been formalized or codified with the addition of rules. A track meet with carefully measured distances, high-tech timing devices, and officials is a very different entity than a lunch-hour race between schoolchildren on a playground. Similarly, a game of ice hockey played inside a rink of known dimensions in the presence of a game clock, scorekeepers, and on-ice officials is not the same as a game of shinny between two teams on a frozen pond. Rules impose structure on sport competitions, thereby creating conditions under which proficiency in physical skills and strategic prowess can be effectively tested between competitors (Torres, 2010). In some instances, the contest is evaluative in nature (e.g., diving or gymnastics where performance is judged against a gold standard), while in other instances, it is comparative (e.g., one team scores more points than another, or an individual racer finishes ahead of all other competitors). As arbiters of these contests, officials play a critical role in upholding both the spirit and the letter of the laws to ensure that all competitors are guaranteed an opportunity to compete and perform in a predictable and safe environment that is both fair and equitable. Those who opt into the role of referee, umpire, or judge – despite constant implicit and explicit challenges to their competence, fairness, and legitimacy in the midst of competition (Simmons, 2011) – must be viewed as competent and committed to performing the job to the best of their abilities while adopting an impartial stance. The significance of this cannot be overstated, for if a sport official is perceived to be lacking in the performance of his or her officiating duties, critique is usually swift to follow.

As you will read in Chapter 2, social constructions, and the narratives that arise from them, of officials as sports' anti-heroes are an age-old phenomenon. The current problem at hand, however, is that these accounts contribute to officiating being increasingly viewed as an undesirable pursuit. For example, incidents of corruption and match fixing at the elite or professional level can be one point of public discussion that jeopardizes the public image and credibility of officials at all levels (Gill, 2013). This is in part due to both the nature of and the speed with which negative portrayals of sport officials are made available to the general public. The rapid evolution of cell phone technology, including high-resolution photo and video capabilities, combined with the popularity of unfiltered on-line social media platforms has served to exponentially amplify both the volume of critiques generated and the speed with which they are disseminated. As an example, a simple search of the World Wide Web using the terms "referee" and "assault" yields thousands of headlines, many of which are inevitably recently reported events. Whether verbal or physical in nature, these assaults are almost always associated with the aggressors' beliefs that the official failed to make the right call or unfairly penalized an athlete or coach in the course of carrying out her or his duties. To be fair, we acknowledge that in some instances these critiques may be accurate – yet in many instances they are not. We also concede that it is a tough job and not everyone will naturally aspire to or have the talent to excel in the role. However, we would equally argue that it is never justifiable, acceptable, or ethical for officials to be angrily demeaned, slandered, threatened, or assaulted by players, coaches, or spectators. The expectation that an official will always be "perfect" in performing their duties, including youth-aged officials just learning their craft, is simply unjust and unrealistic.

Like Bailey Slusher, four out of every five amateur sport officials will tell you that they enter into and enjoy officiating because of their love for the sport (Livingston & Forbes, 2016). This activity, moreover, provides them with a viable way to give back to their sport and to stay connected to others with like interests (Livingston & Forbes, 2017). The social communities that evolve as a result are a source of enjoyment and pleasure. Understanding this is important, for enjoyment or satisfaction is a strong predictor of persistence in sport activities (Boiché & Sarrazin, 2009). Likewise, it should not be surprising that negative commentaries from others, including threats of verbal or physical abuse, rank as the number one reason cited by youth-aged entry-level officials for dropping out (Livingston et al., 2017). Numerous stories in the popular media reinforce this observation; however, such accounts also tend to overgeneralize and suggest the same is true for more experienced officials. In fact, this is rarely the case. Older officials tend to identify family and career demands, or physical limitations caused by age or injury, as the foremost reason for discontinuing their participation. Lack of opportunities for advancement, excessive travel times, and high costs (e.g., registration and insurance fees, equipment) have also been shown to weigh on the decision to quit. Although understudied in comparison to their playing and coaching counterparts, these fresh insights are the product of new theoretical frameworks of inquiry (Chapter 3) and a growing body of evidence on why officials drop out, as well as why they enter into, persist, and thrive in the role. For example, the decision to leave officiating may be influenced by multiple factors as they relate to the individual (e.g., age, experience, gender) (Chapter 4), the task (e.g., demands of a specific sport) (Chapter 5), or the organizational environment (e.g., policies, structures, key actors) in which they are immersed (Chapter 6). Understanding the dynamic interaction between these factors, and being able to effectively address them going forward, will be important if sport organizations hope to stem the problematic rates of officiating attrition observed for various sports around the globe.

Dropping out from the officiating ranks is not a new problem nor is it unique to any given sport. Rather, it is a persistent, pervasive, and global problem and one that Australian researchers have labelled as "...a significant management problem for most sport organizations..." (Cuskelly & Hoye, 2013, p. 451). To put this into context, the magnitude and scope of the problem needs to be considered. For example, the Australian Bureau of Statistics reported an overall decline of 28% in active sport officials from 1993 to 2010 (i.e., from 435,800 to 313,000 individuals, respectively) (Cuskelly & Hoye, 2013). In Canada, these losses were comparably greater, with a 38% decline in active sport officials observed between 1998 and 2010 (i.e., from 937,000 to 582,485, respectively) (Canadian Heritage, 2013; Cuskelly & Hoye, 2013). The shortages created by dropout, moreover, may be compounded by the growth in a sport's popularity or expansion into new countries. In the United States, for example, it is estimated that there will be a 6% increased need for officials by 2028 (U.S. Bureau of Labour Statistics, 2018).

Viewing data from differing sports over the past two decades, at a variety of playing levels, yields equally disheartening results. For example, in 1998 the Dutch volleyball association reported losing 20% of its referees on an annual basis (VanYperen, 1998). Likewise, in the early 2000s, Deacon (2001) noted that 30% of all officials in the Canadian Hockey Association quit every year, as did approximately two-thirds of the new soccer referee recruits in one Canadian province. At about the same time, evidence was emerging out of the United States suggesting that a widespread shortage of officials was forthcoming, with particular challenges beginning to emerge in the sports of field hockey and soccer (Titlebaum, Haberlin, & Titlebaum, 2009). The sport of soccer (or football as it is known in most countries) has a particularly tarnished reputation for the way officials are treated and the resulting attrition that takes place. In England, in an effort to stem attrition and to rebuild its officiating human resources, the English Football Association (FA) launched its "Respect" campaign in 2008 to recruit and retain officials, and early data suggested that it was having the desired response (Parsons & Bairner, 2015). However, in the absence of ongoing research and evaluation, little is known as to whether the short-term successes of such campaigns – with many sports having implemented them in an effort to curb officiating attrition (e.g., Canadian Hockey Association's 1999 "Shared Respect Initiative", Australia's National Rugby League 2016 "Respect Campaign", or Australian Sports Commission's "Year of the Official" 2003) – will prove effective in the long term when it comes to stemming the outflow of officials.

From our perspective, the future of competitive sport demands that sport officials be seen on par with athletes and coaches as necessary participants. Efforts to retain officials, moreover, must be evidence-based, deliberate in effort, and comprehensive in approach. Sport officials are disproportionately underrepresented in sport science research compared to athletes and coaches (MacMahon et al., 2015). Such an investment is minimal at best, yet the good news is that researchers from around the world are now investing more time and effort than ever before in studying this important group of sport participants. In doing so, they are taking stock of what has been studied, while also identifying viable theoretical frameworks, and major information gaps worthy of further study in order to legitimize sport officiating as bona fide field of study (Hancock, Rix-Lièvre, & Côté, 2015). An equally important, yet arguably more immediate and pressing, challenge, however, is for the results of this research to be intentionally and meaningfully mobilized and translated for use by those responsible for supporting the recruitment, retention, development, and advancement of sport officials from the grassroots to professional levels.

In this book, the linkages between these newly emerging research findings and the development, planning, and implementation of multifaceted Officiating Development Programs (ODP) are explored (Chapter 7), while at the same time emphasizing the importance of ongoing research and evaluation in order to assess the effectiveness of such programs (Chapter 8). An ongoing commitment to generating and gathering new evidence through research and evaluation, rather than a reliance on what we think we know and what we have always done, will also be required if we are to effectively stem the current issues faced by sport administrators in the recruitment, retention, development, and advancement of sport officials to their highest levels of performance and effectiveness. Implicit within this is the need to continuously monitor the influence of newly emerging issues within sport (Chapter 9), and the impact – positive or negative – that they may have on the officials' themselves. For example, it is likely that ongoing technological change will continue to impact officials and that the consequences of such change will require new approaches to future research problems.

Importantly, before delving more deeply into all things officiating, it is important to acknowledge that identifying a "one-size-fits-all" officiating solution for all people, sports, and organizations is not achievable, nor advisable. Sport is complex in that it is subject to differing cultural expectations, funding mechanisms, and organizational dynamics, both within and between countries. There are also varying levels of competition (i.e., amateur versus professional, recreational versus competitive), and opportunities for advancement may be distinctly different in highly populated urban versus lesser-populated rural environments. To this end, the purpose of this book is to provide an evidence-based, flexible, and practical guide to those responsible for the recruitment, retention, development, and advancement of amateur-level sport officials. Equipping sport organizations with a deeper understanding and appreciation of officiating will be essential if they are to be enabled to shift their efforts away from activities constantly focused on the recruitment and training of new officials (i.e., a negative quantitative focus) to that of improving the quality of an existing stable officiating corps (i.e., a positive qualitative focus).

TAKE AWAY MESSAGES FROM THIS CHAPTER

- For those that pursue officiating, many do so because of their love for the sport.
- Sports represent games and competitions of physical prowess which have been formalized or codified with the addition of rules.

(Continued)

- Officials play a critical role in upholding both the spirit and the letter of the laws to ensure that all competitors are guaranteed an opportunity to compete and perform in a predictable and safe environment that is both fair and equitable.
- The expectation that an official will always be "perfect" in performing their duties, including youth-aged officials just learning their craft, is simply unrealistic and creates a disproportionate amount of pressure on officials.

Sport Official Dropout

- Attrition from the officiating ranks is a significant sport management problem which is persistent, pervasive, and global in nature.
- Officiating dropout is a product of multiple factors, including those that pertain to the individual, the sport they officiate, and the officiating environment in which they are immersed.

Future Issues and Solutions to Consider

- The future of competitive sport demands that sport officials be seen on par with athletes and coaches as necessary participants within it.
- Efforts to retain officials then must be evidence-based, deliberate in effort, and comprehensive in approach.
- In order to be effective, Officiating Development Programs (ODP) programs must be evidence-based and evaluated on an ongoing basis.
- Identifying a "one-size-fits-all" officiating solution for all people, sports, and organizations is not achievable, nor advisable.

References

Boiché, J.C.S., & Sarrazin, P.G. (2009). Proximal and distal factors associated with dropout versus maintained participation in organized sport. *Journal of Sports Science and Medicine, 8*, 9–16.

Canadian Heritage. (2013). *Sport participation 2010: Research paper.* Ottawa, ON: Government of Canada.

Cuskelly, G., & Hoye, R. (2013). Sports officials' intentions to continue. *Sport Management Review, 16*, 451–464.

Deacon, J. (2001, March 26). Rink rage. *Maclean's, 114(13)*, 20–24.

Gill, R. (2013). AFL umpires: Brand and reputation. *Journal of Sociological Research, 4(2)*, 284–291.

Hancock, D.J., Rix-Lièvre, G., & Côté, J. (2015). Citation network analysis of research on sport officials: A lack of interconnectivity. *International Review of Sport and Exercise Psychology, 8*, 95–105.

Livingston, L.A., & Forbes, S.L. (2016). Factors contributing to the retention of Canadian amateur sport officials: Motivations, perceived organizational support, and resilience. *International Journal of Sports Science & Coaching, 11*, 342–355.

Livingston, L.A., & Forbes, S.L. (2017). Just bounce right back up and dust yourself off: Participation motivations, resilience, and perceived organizational support amongst amateur baseball umpires. *Baseball Research Journal, 46*(2), 91–101.

Livingston, L.A., Forbes, S.L., Wattie, N., Pearson, N., Camacho, T., & Varian, P. (2017). Sport officiating recruitment, development, and retention: A call to action. *Current Issues in Sport Science, 2*, 011. doi: 10.15203/CISS_2017.011.

Parsons, T., & Bairner, A. (2015). You want the buzz of having done well in a game that wasn't easy: A sociological examination of the job commitment of English football referees. *Movement & Sport Sciences, 87*, 41–52.

Simmons, P. (2011). Competent, dependable and respectful: Football refereeing as a model for communicating fairness. *Ethical Space: The International Journal of Communication Ethics, 8*, 33–42.

Titlebaum, P.J., Haberlin, N., & Titlebaum, G. (2009). Recruitment and retention of sports officials. *Recreational Sports Journal, 33*, 102–108.

Torres, C.R. (2010). The danger of selectively changing the rules in youth sport: The case of the strike zone. *JOHPERD, 81*(5), 29–34.

United States Bureau of Labour and Statistics. (2019, September 4). *Umpires, referees, and other sports officials*. Retrieved from https://www.bls.gov/ooh/entertainment-and-sports/umpires-referees-and-other-sports-officials.htm

VanYperen, N.W. (1998). Predicting stay/leave behavior among volleyball referees. *The Sport Psychologist, 12*, 427–439.

Windler, T. (2018). Bailey's shot. *Referee, 43*(4), 64–65.

2 Sociohistorical Construction of Officiating and Officiating Research

"Villains by Necessity"[1] – A Brief Evolution of Sports Officials

Our ability to know how something "comes to be" depends highly on time, place, and resources. Historically, our understanding of sport and its evolution was limited by both the method of record keeping (e.g., oral and written histories) and the value attached to the "thing" at the time. Such is the case for understanding the social and historical evolution of the sports official. Their value is evident from the clues we can glean from exploring the development of sport.

The following section provides a brief primer on how sport officials, sometimes viewed as "villains by necessity", came to be part of the modern sport landscape, as well as why they may have taken on the personae they have. The chapter discussion then shifts to providing a timeline and description of evolving research on officials in sports sciences, identifying trends, and topics of scholarly research about officials' participation, performance, and development.

Historical Origins of Sport and Its Evolution

Numerous ancient cultures had forms of sport and physical activity, such as Sumer, Egypt, Rome, Mesoamerican, and Greece (Crowther, 2007, MacAuley, 1994). However, the Greek or Panhellenic games (e.g., Delphi, Nemea, Isthmia, and Olympia) differed from other ancient activities by holding organized games such as those at Delphi, Nemea, Isthmia, and, most famously, Olympia (MacAuley, 1994). It is this element of organization that lends itself to imposing rules, which allows for the emergence of what we would eventually understand as officiating. However, much like current trends, we know more about the athletes than other participants involved in sport.

As Barney (2004) noted, having someone other than athletes regulating competition is not new. Historical records identify Hellanodikai (Hellanodikas singular) as judges or major officials at the abovementioned Panhellenic games. The Hellanodikai, drawn from elites of Greek society, oversaw the training of athletes prior to competition, determined eligibility and age-class as well as "winners, monitored cheating, and punished those caught violating the rules". In the latter instance, the Hellanodikai were assisted by Alytarchai, who was a leader of the local police force, as well as Rabdouchoi and Mastigophoroi who meted out physical punishment with rods (Golden, 2004). The "officiating" role was embedded in the Panhellenic games dating 580BCE; however, you can see similarities with contemporary officiating crews.

The Panhellenic games influenced Roman culture to a certain degree, as the ancient Olympic games were held in Rome after 80 BCE. Unfortunately, the Games ended in 393 CE, after Christian Emperor Theodosius ordered all pagan-related activities stopped. This edict aligned with Christian beliefs that denounced veneration of the body, as such activities were considered pagan in nature. This move signaled what is historically referred to as the "Dark Ages" (or early Middle Ages), a period where physical activity, especially organized events, was discouraged by the Church (MacAuley, 1994; Ziegler, 2006).

In totality, the Middle Ages (circa 500 CE until approximately 1500 CE) represented a period of heavy religious influence that negated much physical activity outside of that associated with labor (Guttmann, 2000) or was designed for military training under feudal obligation and in the service of the Church (Van Dalen, 2006). Despite proscriptions on sport and games by the Church, such activities continued throughout this time period. Such activities were divided along class lines, with the aristocracy engaging in sports like hunting, archery, fencing, and jousting. Non-aristocracy had game such as folk football (Dunning, 1990). Control of such activities also divided along "class lines" with peasant games highly unregulated, while aristocratic events (e.g., tournaments) were governed by a chivalric code that precluded rule breaking (Olivova, 1981). In the case of this latter group, regulation tended to be self-imposed. This code, which emphasized appropriate behavior, would permeate sport and physical activity during subsequent eras such as the Renaissance (15th and 16th centuries) and the Enlightenment (17th and 18th centuries) (Guttmann, 2000).

Most sports during the Renaissance shifted from "force to finesse" with an increased emphasis on etiquette and propriety (Guttmann, 2000, p. 248). While more evident in the activities of nobility, a similar shift emerged in the sports of commoners. During this period, sports were "more carefully regulated...and much more civilized" than previous periods (Guttmann, 2000, p. 249). The move to regulation continued in the Enlightenment, especially in England, as the development of rules (codification) took hold. For example, the first boxing rules were introduced in 1743. Similarly, the first formalized and recorded cricket rules were created in 1747 (Guttmann, 2000). While there is no evidence of a boxing referee (Standen, 2008), the first set of cricket laws clearly identify an umpire and their responsibilities (Malcolm, 2002). Despite this evidence, history reveals little of the role of sports officials until the 19th century and the emergence of widespread organized sport.

While it is beyond the scope of this chapter to give a full accounting of the evolution of sport, and specifically officiating, it is important to identify three (3) key factors that changed sport irrevocably – *industrialization, modernization,* and *rationalization.* While other factors are also significant in the evolution of modern sport (e.g., British public schools), three particular factors transcend political boundaries. Industrialization, which started in Britain in the late 1700s, involved advancements in manufacturing and had implications for transportation and communication, technology, and leisure time. Industrialization also affected the growth of modern sport in several ways. First, advances in transportation allowed for competition between communities and communication developments allowed for those communities to connect to establish those competitions. Technological advances allowed for the improvement in equipment, as well as artificial lighting. The latter enabled alterations in the work day and led to the development of leisure time (i.e., time away from work). Technological changes were also evident in the sharing of information (e.g., newspapers). The rise of modern sport was a consequence of industrialization (Guttmann, 2000; Vamplew, 2016), whereas global industrialization modernized societies. For sport, this process involved transforming a relatively simple activity that may resemble other games to a more "complex, distinct, and civilized" organized activity (Dunning & Sheard, 1979, p. 86). Written rules are a prerequisite for this process, and with such rules came the necessity for a "third party" to administer them (Dunning & Sheard, 1979). This complexity and standardization of rules reflect elements of what Guttmann (1978) identified as the key attributes of modern sport.

In a critical analysis of the evolution of sport, Guttmann ascribed seven (7) characteristics to what we now recognize as sport. These include secularism (non-religious), equality (i.e., opportunity in competing), specialization (e.g., one-sport athlete with support), rationalization (i.e., implementation of broadly accepted rules), bureaucracy (i.e., governance), quantification (e.g., time, distance, scores), and records (e.g., four-minute mile). Of these characteristics, one is critical for the developing role of the sports official – rationalization. As Guttmann (1978) noted, "... there must be rules of competition ... simply because sports are by definition games, i.e., organized, rule-bound" (p. 40). By the late 1800s, modern sports with its bureaucracy and rules were widespread. The emergence of the sports official was also evident during this period. This was a sports role both embedded in the modern sport system and a "victim" of that modernization process. Increased complexity of sports demanded an arbiter of the rules. However, by the very nature of those rules, they were perceived as "outsiders" (Leslie, 1998). This position in relationship to sport would further transform as sport changed.

Until early 20th century, sport was a means for an individual to participate to the best of one's abilities, to play within an honor code based in trust and fairness, and to build character. This latter element was meant for the participant and those watching. Rules were, for the most part, more about regulating the mechanisms of play (e.g., size of space, equipment). However, with the growth of commercialism and the rise of professional and semi-professional sports, winning became the primary outcome. With this transformation came the need for more prescriptive rules about not only play but also behavior (Cashmore, 2005). The transformation of sport away from an honor-bound pastime to a highly commercialized and professionalized undertaking (at all levels) has significantly affected the role of the official. Today, most officials fulfil the role of "outsider". According to Elias and Scotson (1965), the outsider exists in a relationship with the "established" based on a power relation. Established groups (e.g., athletes, coaches) are readily identifiable, demonstrate more intra-group cohesion, have well-established networks, and exercise significant power within their sport. Officials, in contrast, stand on the edge of sport (literally and figuratively in many cases), part of the action, but are arguably never really wholly accepted as part of the group. Officials understand the context and the general participation goals and interests of other participants, but historically have been rarely, if ever, treated as participants themselves. As Mennell (1992) noted, "...outsiders identify with and understand the established better than the established do the outsiders" (as cited in Liston, 2005, p. 27).

This isolation of officials also bears out in other ways. As Nosal (2015) noted, there are fewer officials than players, so it's easier to focus on them and lay blame for poor performance at their feet. Expectation for error-less performance in sport officials' performance carries much weight compared to their athletic counterparts (Simmons & Cunningham, 2013) where error is something more accepted and normalized part of skill development. As noted above, officials often operate outside and around the physical context of the activity, and their very appearance sets them visually apart (e.g., striped or colored shirts). Officials are often one of the few, if not the only ones, who truly understand the rules but are subjected to multiple interpretations by those who play, coach, and watch. Additionally, their very decisions put them in the middle as they render decisions for one side/player versus the other. This marginalization, or outsider perspective of officials, also permeated the sport research landscape until more recently, as the next section will further illuminate and address. Questions remain about ways social identities are developed and preserved in the larger society, and ways this social perception act on officials' self-perception and social identity, including the implications this has for recruitment, development, and retention.

Evolution of Sports Officiating Research

The evolution of research on sports officiating, while lagging behind other sport-related research, emerged from a maelstrom created in the wake of the Cold War that resulted in the scientization of education in western nations (Forbes & Livingston, 2012). This emergence was earmarked by a "redefining" of the field by deemphasizing the pedagogical nature of physical education in favor of a greater focus on developing and sustaining academic disciplines that were more closely aligned with their parent disciplines (e.g., psychology, sociology, history, and their respective subdisciplines within the sport context). Research on sport and physical activity in the 1970s was dominated by a focus on the nature of the discipline, as well as the organizational structure of the fields (Corbin, 1993).

The 1980s reflected "a time of identity seeking" (Corbin, 1993, p. 84) wherein the scientization of the Cold War era continued through efforts to make a "better athlete", thereby supporting sport-related research. This was clearly evident in the Canadian context as government financial support poured into the expansion of post-secondary physical education/kinesiology programs populated by researchers focused on sports studies. This support came through the Canada Applied Sport Research Grants Program and provided enhanced credibility for emerging programs and specialities (Forbes & Livingston, 2012; Macintosh & Whitson, 1990). This expansion of the research agenda was accompanied by growth in graduate programs and the development of specialized subdisciplines.

The ongoing "scientization" of these programs was clearly evident in the form and focus on officiating scholarly works. Growth in sports-related research was also evident in the area of sports officiating; however, the scope and focus were predominantly psychological in nature. The early officiating studies focused on officials' consistency (Alker, Straub, & Leary, 1973), personality (Fratzke, 1975), and psychological profiles (Kroll, 1977). Research starting in the 1980s and into the 2000s saw a diversification of sport official research spurred by increased inquiries into sources of stress experienced by officials in their role (Anshel & Weinberg, 1995, 1999; Goldsmith & Williams, 1992; Kaissidis-Rodnafinos, Anshel, & Porter, 1997; Kaissidis-Rodnafinos, Anshel, & Sideridis, 1998; Nesti & Sewell, 1999; Rainey, 1995; Rainey & Cherilla, 1993; Rainey & Hardy, 1997, 1999; Stewart & Ellery, 1996, 1998; Taylor, Daniel, Leith, & Burke, 1990). Most of the literature from this period surmised that stress and the difficulties in managing it (i.e., coping) were significant contributors to officiating dropout. While important to research progress, these early investigations into the officials' role focused predominantly on their psychological traits and susceptibility to officiating pressures. However, stress-research on sport officials later summarized in these studies that official's actually report only low to moderate stress levels (Rainey & Winterich, 1995).

Compared to research on other specialized sports-related topics, officiating scholarship still lagged behind. However, by the late 1990s and into the early 2000s, an increase in officiating research occurred wherein scholars clearly looked to work being done in other areas. Particularly, a predominant theme became understanding officials' decision-making and related processes (e.g., decision bias) that impacted officiating performance (e.g., Auweele, Boen, De Geest, & Freys, 2004; Dennis, Carron, & Loughheed, 2002; Helsen & Bultynck, 2004; Jones, Paull, & Eskine, 2002; Lane, Nevill, Ahmad, & Balmer, 2006; MacMahon & Ste-Marie, 2002; Mascarenhas, Collins, & Mortimer, 2002; Nevill, Balmer, & Williams, 2002; Philippe, Vallerand, Andrianarisoa, & Brunel, 2009; Proios & Doganis, 2003; Souchon, Coulomg-Cabagno, Traclet, & Rascle, 2004; Ste-Marie, 1999, Ste-Marie & Lee, 1991; Sutter & Kocher, 2004). A recognized lack of interconnectivity in officiating study has been pointed out (where personality, stress, and decision-making factors are more commonly studied, Hancock, Rix-Lièvre, & Côté, 2015).

Similarly, performance-related studies examining physiological aspects of officiating emerged around the same time. For example, Wilkins, Petersen, and Quinney (1991) used time-motion analysis, coupled with heart rate monitors, to assess physiological stress on hockey officials. Other studies also explored analogous physiological performance factors in game settings (e.g., Castagna, Abt, & D'Ottavio, 2007; Galanti et al., 2008; Kay & Gill, 2003, 2004; Krustup et al., 2009; Leicht, 2004; Martin, Smith, Tolfrey, & Jones, 2001; Weston, Castagna, Helsen, & Impellizzeri, 2009; Weston Castagna, Impellizzeri, Rampinini, & Breivik, 2010).

While psychological and physiological studies contributed the bulk of officiating-related research from the 1980s into the early 2000s, other less robust areas emerged. For example, a few studies pursued analysis of the relationship between injury and rules enforcement and quality of officiating (Andersen, Engebretsen, & Bahr, 2004; Collins, Fields, & Comstok, 2008; Livingston & Forbes, 2000, 2003; Parayre, 1989; Watson & Rickwood, 1999). There was also some early work in the area of entry and continuance of amateur sports officials; however, this topic would not be taken up again until the mid-2000s (Furst, 1991; Ross & Vaughn, 1995). What is evident in these early studies is an overwhelming emphasis on the individual official with little consideration of the context in which they carry out their roles. Additionally, most studies focused on single, specific sports (e.g., football/soccer) with little consideration of cross-sport similarities and were not multidisciplinary in nature.

A recent analysis of the history of studies on sport officials provides a picture of where interest has been and needs to be. Hancock, Miller, Roaten, Chapman, and Stanley (2019) comprehensively analyzed 386 officiating research studies that took place between 1970 and 2018. First, they found that women officials received relatively limited attention compared to male officials (12% versus 43%, respectively), while close to half of the studies (45%) included both male and female officials (based on studies that reported officials' sex). Second, "interactor" type (or team-based, invasion game) officials (e.g., football, basketball, rugby) made up 82% of studies, with European football accounting for 57% of that total – and basketball next with 12%. Professional, international, and national sport officials were most involved, covering 77% of studies. More crucially, retention and official development topics only appeared in 10% of the studies, with even less attention directed to burnout, female officials, communication, and officiating groups (i.e., crews, teams), making up a modest 7% of studies. In sum, Hancock et al.'s (2019) useful findings demonstrate a need for further understanding about female officials' experiences, community and novice officiating levels, sports other than team/invasion games (i.e., "interactor" officiating settings), and psycho-social factors gaining interest, including officials' mental health (Goutte-barge, Johnson, Rochcongar, Rosier, & Kerkhoffs, 2017; Kilic, Johnson, Kerkhoffs, Rosier, & Gouttebarge, 2018), communication and interaction (Cunningham, Simmons, & Mascarenhas, 2018; Furley & Schweizer, 2016), and officiating team processes (Boyer, MacMahon, Récopé, & Rix-Lièvre, 2020; Hancock, Martin, Paradis, & Evans, 2018).

Current research still explores physiological and psychological domains, such as self-efficacy (Myers et al., 2012), resilience (Livingston & Forbes, 2016), key attributes of elite officials (Morris & O'Connor, 2017), and impact of physical workload and training practices (Leicht et al., 2019). However, new areas of research are emerging which reflect a change in perception related to the role officials play in sports. One new area centers on decision-making in officiating, and not only how decisions are made, but where officials are physically situated in relation to that action, as well as what they are looking at and what cognitive processes are going on (for review see Raab, Bar-Eli, Plessner, & Araújo, 2019). Another area considers how "home advantage" may also influence decisions made by officials (Dawson, Massey, & Downward, 2019). One additional and potentially litigious area of study is the relationship between officiating and sports-related injuries. We are also seeing a reemergence of sociocultural and economics studies. For example, several new works explore historical and philosophical examination of officiating. While not all areas are relevant to the context of this book, they do speak to growing recognition of officials as key members of the sporting context.

A new thrust in performance-based officiating research is how we can train decision-making to "improve" the quality of officiating (Gulec, Yilmaz, Isler, O'Connor, & Clarke, 2019; Schweizer, Plessner, Kahlert, & Brand, 2011). The use of technology (an "emerging issue" facing sport officials is discussed in greater detail in Chapter 9) has emerged in tandem with decision-making. Studies have explored how technology can influence how officials process their environment (e.g., 360 degree VR; Kittel, Larkin, Elsworthy, & Spittle, 2019a). Researchers are also looking at how technology can be used to evaluate officiating performance (i.e., decision-making skills assessment tools; Kittel, Larkin, Elsworthy, & Spittle, 2019b).

While the research foci noted above tend to follow traditional research approaches (e.g., centered predominantly on the individual), other emergent research recognizes an important environmental constraint on sport officials with more administrative focus – perceived organizational support (POS). As discussed elsewhere, POS relates to the role organizations can play with respect to supporting officials on their developmental pathways (Livingston et al., 2017). Of related relevance is the officials' perception of this support (Livingston & Forbes, 2016). New areas include gender issues in officiating (Kim & Hong, 2016; Reid & Dallaire, 2019; Schaeperkoetter, 2017) and positive factors associated with officiating retention (Mack, Schulenkorf, Adair, & Bennie, 2018). Additionally, researchers have expanded their focus by moving beyond the elite sports to explore officiating in the context of youth sports (Ridinger, 2015). Others are examining ways to understand retention factors better (see Illardi, 2018; Jordan, Upright, & Forsythe, 2019; Ridinger et al, 2017). The recent explosion of officiating-related research, along with the change in focus, bodes well for being able to understand and support officials. This work also serves notice that sports officials are now starting to move away from outsider status.

TAKE AWAY MESSAGES FROM THIS CHAPTER

- Officiating roles have evolved alongside sports' own structural changes and cultural history.
- An official's place in sport needs to be neutral and impartial. However, this does not mean they are not part of the larger landscape of sport.
- The prevailing culture of sport has systemically marginalized officials (us versus them).
- Obfuscating, and vilification of, the necessary role officials occupy ultimately can compromise athletic performance.
- Early research focused on the individual official, stripping away any organizational context that may impact their performance and persistence. Administrators can reverse this trend by including and supporting officials.
- Retention and development, female official experiences, non-team-based sports, and psychosocial factors, such as mental health, communication, and officiating crews/teams, are understudied. Increased attention on these issues will be a task for academics and practitioners alike in the future.

Note

1 William Shakespeare: King Lear, Act I, Scene II.

References

Alker, H.A., Straub, W.F., & Leary, J. (1973). Achieving consistency: A study of basketball officiating. *Journal of Vocational Behavior, 3*, 335–343.

Andersen, T.E., Engebretsen, L., & Bahr, R. (2004). Rules violations as a cause of injuries in male Norwegian professional football: Are the referees doing their job? *American Journal of Sports Medicine, 32*, 62S–8S

Anshel, M.H., & Weinberg, R.S. (1995). Sources of acute stress in American and Australian basketball referees. *Journal of Applied Sport Psychology, 7*, 11–22.

Auweele, Y.V., Boen, F., De Geest, A., & Feys, J. (2004). Judging bias in Synchronized Swimming: Open feedback leads to nonperformance-based conformity. *Journal of Sport & Exercise Psychology, 26*, 561–71.

Boyer, S., MacMahon, C., Récopé, M., & Rix-Lièvre, G. (2020). The assistant referees' activity in refereeing elite football: Preoccupations when not judging offside. *Psychology of Sport and Exercise, 48*, 101662. doi: 10.1016/j.psychsport.2020.101662

Cashmore, E. (2005). *Making sense of sports*. London: Routledge.

Castagna, C., Abt, G., & D'Ottavio, S. (2007). Physiological aspects of soccer refereeing performance and training. *Sports Medicine, 37*, 625–646.

Collins, C.L., Fields, S.K., & Comstock, R.D. (2008). When the rules of the game are broken: What proportion of high school sports-related injuries are related to illegal activity? *Injury Prevention, 14*, 34–8.

Corbin, C.B. (1993). The field of physical education: Common goals, not common roles. *Journal of Physical Education, Recreation & Dance, 64*(1), 79–87.

Crowther, N.B. (2007). *Sport in ancient times*. Westport, CT: Greenwood Publishing Group.

Cunningham, I., Simmons, P., & Mascarenhas, D. (2018). Sport officials' strategies for managing interactions with players: Face-work on the front-stage. *Psychology of Sport and Exercise, 39*, 154–162.

Dawson, P., Massey, P., & Downward, P. (2019). Television match officials, referees, and home advantage: Evidence from the European rugby cup. *Sport Management Review*.

Dennis, P.W., Carron, A.V., & Loughead, T.M. (2002). The relationship between game location and decisions by national hockey league officials. *Avante, 8*, 67–73.

Dunning, E. (1990). Sociological reflections on sport, violence and civilization. *International Review for the Sociology of Sport, 25*(1), 65–81.

Dunning, E., & Sheard, K. (1979). *Barbarians, gentlemen and players: A sociological study of the development of rugby football*. Australian National University Press. Retrieved from https://openresearch-repository.anu.edu.au/bitstream/1885/115193/2/b12248885.pdf

Eder, P., & Eisenberger, R. (2008). Perceived organizational support: Reducing the negative influence of coworker withdrawal behavior. *Journal of Management, 34*, 55–68.

Eisenberger, R., Huntington, R., Hutchison, S., & Sowa, D. (1986). Perceived organizational support. *Journal of Applied Psychology, 71,* 500–7.

Elias, N., & Scotson, J. (1965). *The established and the outsiders.* London: Frank Cass.

Forbes, S., & Livingston, L. (2012). Roots, rifts, and reorientations: Rediscovering the common community of inquiry. In E. Singleton, & A. Varpalotai, *Pedagogy in motion–A community of inquiry for human movement studies.* (pp. 45–63). London, ON: Althouse Press.

Fratzke, M.R. (1975). Personality and biographical traits of superior and average college basketball officials. *The Research Quarterly, 46,* 484–488.

Furley, P., & Schweizer, G. (2016). Nonverbal communication of confidence in soccer referees: An experimental test of Darwin's leakage hypothesis. *Journal of Sport and Exercise Psychology, 38*(6), 590–597.

Furst, D.M. (1991). Career contingencies: Patterns of initial entry and continuity in collegiate sports officiating. *Journal of Sport Behavior, 14,* 93–102.

Galanti, G., Pizzi, A., Lucarelli, M., Stefani, L., Gianassi, M., Di Tante, V., Toncelli, L., Moretti, A., & Del Furia, F. (2008). The cardiovascular profile of soccer referees: An echocardiographic study. *Cardiovascular Ultrasound, 6,* 8–12.

Goldsmith, P. A., & Williams, J. M. (1992). Perceived stressors for football and volleyball officials from three rating levels. *Journal of Sport Behavior, 15*(2), 106–118.

Gouttebarge, V., Johnson, U., Rochcongar, P., Rosier, P., & Kerkhoffs, G. (2017). Symptoms of common mental disorders among professional football referees: A one-season prospective study across Europe. *The Physician and Sportsmedicine, 45*(1), 11–16.

Gulec, U., Yilmaz, M., Isler, V., O'Connor, R.V., & Clarke, P.M. (2019). A 3D virtual environment for training soccer referees. *Computer Standards & Interfaces, 64,* 1–10.

Guttmann, A. (1978). *From ritual to record: The nature of modern sports.* New York, NY: Columbia University Press.

Guttmann, A. (2000). The development of modern sports. In J.J. Coakley & E. Dunning (Eds.), *Handbook of sports studies* (pp. 248–259). Newbury Park, CA: Sage Publications Ltd.

Hancock, D.J., Martin, L.J., Paradis, K.F., & Evans, M.B. (2018). Exploring perceptions of group processes in ice hockey officiating. *Journal of Applied Sport Psychology, 30,* 222–240.

Hancock, D.J., Miller, S., Roaten. H., Chapman, K., & Stanley, C. (2019, July). An analysis of literature on sport officiating research. Presentation at the *European Federation of Sport and Exercise Psychology Congress.* University of Münster, Germany.

Hancock, D.J., Rix-Lièvre, G., & Côté, J. (2015). Citation network analysis of research on sport officials: A lack of interconnectivity. *International Review of Sport and Exercise Psychology, 8*(1), 95–105.

Helsen, W., & Bultynck, J.B. (2004). Physical and perceptual-cognitive demands of top-class refereeing in association football. *Journal of Sports Sciences, 22,* 179–89.

Hickey, C.F. (2004). Pathfinding and pathmaking: J.A Mangan and imperialism, education and socialization. In *Serious Sport* (pp. 59–79). New York, NY: Routledge.

Ilardi, R. (2018). Factors that affect retention of sport officials (*Master's thesis*, The College at Brockport, State University of New York, U.S.A). Available from https://digitalcommons.brockport.edu/pes_synthesis/49

Jones, M.V., Paull, G.C., & Erskine, J. (2002). The impact of a team's aggressive reputation on the decisions of association football referees. *Journal of Sports Sciences, 20,* 991–1000.

Jordan, P., Upright, P., & Forsythe, S. (2019). Rural Kentucky sport officials' perspectives on recruitment, training and retention. *KAHPERD Journal, 56*(2), 59–72.

Kay, B., & Gill, N.D. (2003). Physical demands of elite rugby league referees, part one: Time and Motion Analysis. *Journal of Science and Medicine in Sport, 6,* 339–42.

Kay, B., & Gill, N.D. (2004). Physical demands of elite rugby league referees, part two: Heart rate responses and implications for training and fitness testing. *Journal of Science and Medicine in Sport, 7,* 165–73.

Kaissidis-Rodafinos, A., Anshel, M.H., & Porter, A. (1997). Personal and situational factors that predict coping strategies for acute stress among basketball referees. *Journal of Sports Sciences, 15*(4), 427–436.

Kaissidis-Rodafinos, A., Anshel, M.H., Sideridis, G. (1998) Sources, intensity, and responses to stress in Greek and Australian basketball referees. *International Journal of Sport Psychology, 29,* 1–22.

Kilic, Ö., Johnson, U., Kerkhoffs, G.M., Rosier, P., & Gouttebarge, V. (2018). Exposure to physical and psychosocial stressors in relation to symptoms of common mental disorders among European professional football referees: A prospective cohort study. *BMJ Open Sport & Exercise Medicine, 4*(1), e000306.

Kim, M.C., & Hong, E. (2016). A red card for women: Female officials ostracized in South Korean football. *Asian Journal of Women's Studies, 22*(2), 114–130.

Kittel, A., Larkin, P., Elsworthy, N., & Spittle, M. (2019a). Using 360° virtual reality as a decision-making assessment tool in sport. *Journal of Science and Medicine in Sport, 22*(9), 1049–53.

Kittel, A., Larkin, P., Elsworthy, N., & Spittle, M. (2019b). Video-based testing in sporting officials: A systematic review. *Psychology of Sport and Exercise.*

Kroll, W. (1977). Psychological scaling of AIAW code-of-ethics for officials and spectators. 12 *The Research Quarterly, 48,* 475–479.

Krustup, P., Helsen, W., Randers, M.B., Christensen, J.F., MacDonald, C., Rebelo, A.N., & Bangsbo, J. (2009). Activity profile and physical demands of football referees and assistant referees in international games. *Journal of Sports Sciences, 27,* 1167–1176.

Lane, A.M., Nevill, A.M., Ahmad, N.S., & Balmer, N. (2006). Soccer referee decision-making: "Shall I Blow the Whistle?"'. *Journal of Sports Science and Medicine, 5,* 243–253.

Leicht, A.S. (2004). Cardiovascular stress on an elite basketball referee during national competition. *British Journal of Sports Medicine, 38,* E10–E11.

Leicht, A.S., Fox, J., Connor, J., Sargent, C., Sinclair, W., Stanton, R., & Scanlan, A. (2019). External activity demands differ between referees and players during a sub-elite, men's basketball match. *Research Quarterly for Exercise and Sport, 90*(4), 1–6.

Leslie, J.P. (1998). The evangeline league's man in the blue serge suit: Trials and tribulations. *Louisiana History, 39*(2), 167–188.

Liston, K. (2005). Established-outsider relations between males and females in male-associated sports in Ireland. *European Journal for Sport and Society, 2*(1), 25–33.

Liston, K. (2011). Sport and leisure. *The Sociological Review, 59,* 160–180.

Livingston, L.A., & Forbes, S.L. (2000). Rule changes, rule enforcement, and ocular injury rates in women's lacrosse and men's ice hockey. *International Journal of Sports Vision, 6,* 37–50.

Livingston, L.A., & Forbes, S.L. (2003). Rule modification and strict rule enforcement as a means of reducing injury in invasion games? *Avante, 8,* 12–20.

Livingston, L.A., & Forbes, S.L. (2016). Factors contributing to the retention of Canadian amateur sport officials: Motivations, perceived organizational support, and resilience. *International Journal of Sports Science & Coaching, 11*(3), 342–355.

Livingston, L.A., Forbes, S.L., Wattie, N., Pearson, N., Camacho, T., & Varian, P. (2017). Sport officiating recruitment, development, and retention: A call to action. *Current Issues in Sport Science (CISS).* 2:011. doi: 10.15203/ CISS_2017.011

MacAuley, D. (1994). A history of physical activity, health and medicine. *Journal of the Royal Society of Medicine, 87*(1), 32–5.

Mack, M., Schulenkorf, N., Adair, D., & Bennie, A. (2018). Factors influencing the development of elite-level sports officials in Australia: The AFL, ABA and FFA. *Sport in Society, 21*(9), 1240–1257.

MacMahon, C., & Ste-Marie, D.M. (2002). Decision-making by experienced rugby referees: Use of perceptual information and episodic memory. *Perceptual and Motor Skills, 95*(2), 570–572.

Malcolm, D. (2002). Cricket and civilizing processes: A response to Stokvis. *International Review for the Sociology of Sport, 37*(1), 37–57.

Martin, J., Smith, N.C., Tolfrey, K., & Jones, A.M. (2001). Activity analysis of English premiership rugby football union refereeing. *Ergonomics, 44,* 1069–1075.

Macintosh, D., & Whitson, D. (1990). *Game planners: Transforming Canada's sport system.* McGill-Queen's Press-MQUP.

Mascarenhas, D.R.D., Collins, D., & Mortimer, P. (2002). The art of reason versus the exactness of science in elite refereeing: Comments on Plessner and Betsch. *Journal of Sport & Exercise Psychology, 24,* 328–33.

Mennell, S. (1992). *Norbert Elias.* Oxford: Blackwell.

Morris, G., & O'Connor, D. (2017). Key attributes of expert NRL referees. *Journal of Sports Sciences, 35*(9), 852–857.

Myers, N.D., Feltz, D.L., Guillén, F., & Dithurbide, L. (2012). Development of, and initial validity evidence for, the reference self-efficacy scale: A multistudy report. *Journal of Sport & Exercise Psychology, 34,* 737–765.

Nesti, M., & Sewell, D. (1999). Losing it: The importance of anxiety and mood stability in sport. *Journal of Personal & Interpersonal Loss, 4*(3), 257–268.

Nevill, A.M., Balmer, N.J., & Williams, A.M. (2002). The influence of crowd noise and experience upon refereeing decisions in football. *Psychology of Sport and Exercise, 3,* 261–272.

Nosal, P. (2015). Sport catalogue of the others: 'The Otherness' as a perspective in social sport. *Miscellanea Anthropologica et Sociologica, 16*(4), 15–30.

Olivova, V. (1981). From the arts of chivalry to gymnastics. *Canadian Journal of History of Sport, 12*(2), 29–55.

Parayre, R. (1989). The effect of rules and officiating on the occurrence and prevention of Injuries. In C.R. Castaldi & E.F. Hoerner (Eds.), *Safety in ice hockey ASTM STP 1050* (pp. 37–43). Philadelphia, PA: American Society for Testing and Materials.

Philippe, F.L., Vallerand, R.J., Andrianarisoa, J., & Brunel, P. (2009). Passion in referees: Examining their affective and cognitive experiences in sport situations. *Journal of Sport & Exercise Psychology, 31*, 77–96.

Proios, M., & Doganis, G. (2003). Experiences from active membership and participation in decision making processes and age in moral reasoning and goal orientation of referees. *Perceptual and Motor Skills, 96*(1), 113–26.

Raab, M., Bar-Eli, M., Plessner, H., & Araújo, D. (2019). The past, present and future of research on judgment and decision making in sport. *Psychology of Sport and Exercise, 42*, 25–32.

Rainey, D. W. (1995). Stress, burnout, and intention to terminate among umpires. *Journal of Sport Behavior, 18*(4), 312–323.

Rainey, D. W., & Cherilla, K. (1993). Conflict with baseball umpires: An observational study. *Journal of Sport Behavior, 16*(1), 49–59.

Rainey, D. W., & Hardy, L. (1997). Ratings of stress by rugby referees. *Perceptual and Motor Skills, 84*(3), 728–730.

Rainey, D. W., & Hardy, L. (1999). Sources of stress, burnout and intention to terminate among rugby union referees. *Journal of Sports Sciences, 17*(10), 797–806.

Rainey, D., & Winterich, D. (1995). Magnitude of stress reported by basketball referees. *Perceptual and Motor Skills, 81*(3_suppl), 1241–1242.

Ridinger, L.L. (2015). Contributors and constraints to involvement with youth sports officiating. *Journal of Amateur Sport, 1*(2), 103–127.

Reid, K., & Dallaire, C. (2019). "Because there are so few of us": The marginalization of female soccer referees in Ontario, Canada. *Women in Sport and Physical Activity Journal, 27*(1), 12–20.

Ridinger, L.L., Kim, K.R., Warner, S., & Tingle, J.K. (2017). Development of the referee retention scale. *Journal of Sport Management, 31*(5), 514–527.

Ross, C.M., & Vaughn, T. (1995, Spring). Strategies for successfully recruiting and retaining quality intramural sports officials. *NIRSA Journal, 19*, 16–19.

Schaeperkoetter, C.C. (2017). Basketball officiating as a gendered arena: An autoethnography. *Sport Management Review, 20*(1), 128–141.

Schweizer, G., Plessner, H., Kahlert, D., & Brand, R. (2011). A video-based training method for improving soccer referees' intuitive decision-making skills. *Journal of Applied Sport Psychology, 23*(4), 429–442.

Simmons, P., & Cunningham, I. (2013). Communication and sport officials. In P.M. Pedersen (Ed.), *Routledge Handbook of Sport Communication* (pp. 461–470).

Souchon, N., Coulomb-Cabagno, G., Traclet, A., & Rascle, O. (2004). Referees decision making in handball and transgressive behaviors: Influence of stereotypes about gender of players? *Sex Roles, 5*, 445–453.

Standen, J. (2008). The manly sports: The problematic use of criminal law to regulate sports violence. *Journal Criminal Law & Criminology, 99*, 619.

Stewart, M. J., & Ellery, P. J. (1996). Amount of psychological stress reported by high school volleyball officials. *Perceptual and Motor Skills, 83*(1), 337–338.

Stewart, M.J., & Ellery, P.J. (1998). Sources and magnitude of perceived psychological stress in high school volleyball officials. *Perceptual and Motor Skills, 87*, 1275–1282.

Ste-Marie, D.M. (1999). Expert-novice differences in gymnastic judging: An information-processing perspective. *Applied Cognitive Psychology, 13*, 269–281.

Ste-Marie, D.M., & Lee, T.D. (1991). Prior processing effects on gymnastic judging. *Journal of Experimental Psychology – Learning Memory and Cognition, 17*, 26–36.

Sutter, M., & Kocher, M.G. (2004). Favortism of agents: The case of referees, home bias. *Journal of Economic Psychology, 25*, 461–469.

Taylor, A. H., Daniel, J. V., Leith, L., & Burke, R. J. (1990). Perceived stress, psychological burnout and paths to turnover intentions among sport officials. *Journal of Applied Sport Psychology, 2*(1), 84–97.

Vamplew, W. (2016). Sport, industry and industrial sport in Britain before 1914: Review and revision. *Sport in Society, 19*(3), 340–355.

Van Dalen, D.B. (2006). Preamble: The idea of history of physical education during the middle ages and renaissance. In E.F. Zeigler (Ed.), *Sport and Physical Education in the Middle Ages*. Bloomington, ID: Trafford.

Watson, R., & Rickwood, G.D. (1999). Stewards of ice hockey: A historical review of safety rules in Canadian Amateur ice hockey. *Sport History Review, 30*, 27–38.

Weston, M., Castagna, C., Helsen, W., & Impellizzeri, F.M., (2009). Relationship among field-test measures and physical match performance in elite-standard soccer referees. *Journal of Sports Sciences, 17*, 1177–1184.

Weston, M., Castagna, C., Impellizzeri, F.M., Rampinini, E., & Breivik, S. (2010). Ageing and physical match performance in English premier league soccer referees. *Journal of Science and Medicine in Sport, 13*, 96–100.

Wilkins, H.A., Petersen, S.R., & Quinney, H.A. (1991). Time-motion analysis of and heart rate responses to amateur ice hockey officiating. *Canadian Journal of Sport Sciences, 16*, 302–307.

Ziegler, E.F. (2006). *Sport and physical education in the middle ages.* Bloomington, IN: Trafford.

3   A Conceptual Framework for the Study of Sport Officials

As the aphorism goes, there is "nothing quite like a good theory" (Lewin, 1951). Moreover, the need for sound theory is particularly important in an expanding area of research (see Livingston et al., 2017) to identify gaps, interpret findings, and guide future research. We feel that for sport science research on officials to advance, a sound and comprehensive theoretical framework is needed to guide that process.

The purpose of this chapter is to propose a conceptual framework to help better understand the factors that influence the development and performance of officials. In turn, by establishing a rigorous base for explaining the complex demands on officials, it can contribute practical utility for framing strategic planning and program implementation and evaluation of officiating management agendas. To be clear, the framework we describe below is not intended to be a definitive model for officiating or for the development of sport officials. Rather, the goal is to provide a framework and set of characteristics that researchers and practitioners can use to (i) evaluate and guide research (see Rienhoff, Tirp, Strauß, Baker, & Schorer, 2016; Webdale, Baker, Schorer, & Wattie, 2019) and (ii) provide a toolkit for considering the combinations of factors relevant to officiating on sport-by-sport basis. Ultimately, this chapter aims to serve as a proof of concept for a constraints-based framework for understanding officiating, and as a primer for subsequent chapters.

Why a New Framework and Theory?

This is a fair question. Given the existence of theoretical frameworks and models that currently exist for athlete development, and for officiating performance, why do we propose an alternative? Although a number of models and theoretical frameworks for *athlete* development exist (e.g., The Foundations, Talent, Elite & Mastery (FTEM) model: Gulbin, Croser, Morley, & Weissensteiner, 2013; the Developmental Model of Sport Participation (DMSP): Côté, Baker, & Abernethy, 2007; Côté & Fraser-Thomas, 2016), it is not clear at this point in time if it is appropriate to simply adopt athlete-specific frameworks given that certain areas of officiating research are still emerging (although we do believe the FTEM should be considered as strong candidate; see Chapter 7). Furthermore, some of these models are largely stage-based models that describe the developmental activities specific to athlete participation (see Baker & Wattie, in press for a review). In some cases, these models center around developmental activities that are so specific to athlete participation (e.g., DMSP), that they are likely too restrictive to be of use in the context of sport officiating. They are also not ecological in the sense that they fail to accommodate the influence of important environmental factors, which we argue is necessary for understanding the development and performance of sport officials.

Similarly, there are models for officiating performance that already exist. Plessner and MacMahon (2013) proposed a taxonomy based on the demands of officiating different sports. This framework describes officials along two continuums, based on degree of movement and interaction with athletes, as well as the perceptual-cognitive demands (number of external cues and athletes monitored). Mascarenhas, Collins, and Mortimer's (2005) Cornerstones Performance Model of Refereeing similarly describes the skills and abilities required for successful officiating performance. Specifically, this model describes successful officiating performance as the product of (i) knowledge and application of the law (i.e., rules), (ii) contextual judgment, (iii) personality and game management skills, and (iv) fitness, positioning, and mechanics (Mascarenhas et al., 2005). This model has proven very useful in the context of training officials in soccer and rugby, and has relevance to many other team and invasion sports. Naturally, however, the weight of each component depends sport-specific task constraints (see Chapter 5). Other modelling of successful officiating has addressed communication performance – what Mascarenhas et al. (2005) originally described as 'personality and game management' – as a combination of personal qualities, impression management, social monitoring, and interaction skills in team sport officials (Cunningham, Simmons, Mascarenhas, & Redhead, 2014). While the model's development included a variety of team-based 'interactor' sports (MacMahon & Plessner, 2013), it can similarly reflect a categorization of communication performance factors that does not account for task-environment constraints of different sports.

While Plessner and MacMahon's (2013) taxonomy and the Cornerstones model (Mascarenhas et al., 2005) have each made important theoretical and applied contributions to our understanding of sport officiating, we propose that these models do not explicitly account for other important factors that influence officials' performance and learning. First, like many athlete development models, these models do not account for the important role of environmental factors. Nor do they account for officials' individual characteristics and the meaningful influence they can have. As such, a framework to guide future research needs to include elements that represent environmental forces.

These models also predominantly emphasize *performance*, specifically the task demands, and skills and abilities needed for successful performance. They do not have components for understanding other outcomes like recruitment, retention, and attrition, and development. Some of these areas of research, like the development of sport officials, require considerable attention (Pina, Passos, Araújo, & Maynard, 2018). Last, the Cornerstones model arguably emphasizes the 'micro-structure' of practice activities (specific skills and drills: See Güllich, 2019). Although the micro-structure of practice activities is incredibly important, it is difficult to conceptualize how the macro-structure (participation and practice histories across developmental levels and between expertise levels) is incorporated into such a model. In Chapter 7, we discuss the importance of macro-structures on the development of sport officials.

We propose that understanding the broader range of topics and outcomes in the officiating literature requires a more ecological, multidimensional approach. This notion is not particularly novel. Indeed, a study of excellence in English Premier League (EPL) soccer referees (Slack, Maynard, Butt, & Olusoga, 2013) supports the need for an ecological approach that recognizes the ways physical, environmental, and psychological factors intersect in official development and research. Other studies highlight the importance of individual-environment interactions (i.e., ecological dynamics) in officials' decision-making behavior and performance. Specifically, officiating decision-making is said to be an 'emergent process' during invasion games where officials not only need to satisfy, first, overarching imperatives, such as to maintain game control and preserve "game integrity", but also meet expectations for safety, fairness, accuracy, and entertainment (Russell, Renshaw, & Davis, 2019). Indeed, an ecological viewpoint has become the basis of new concepts that interpret officiating performance and game activities as a 'co-constructed' product with the players (Cunningham, Mascarenhas, Simmons, & Rix-Lièvre, under review; Rix-Lièvre, Boyer, Terfous, Coutarel, & Lièvre, 2015; Russell, Renshaw, & Davids, 2019). These ecological-based explanations attempt to account for ways officials construct their performance and types of contributing and influencing factors and constraints on their performance.

Similarly, this positioning of officiating performance in its ecology has also been applied to officiating developmental perspectives. Suggestions from within the officiating field recommend a shift from "phase-like", stage modelling of officiating development that might be unrealistic and sometimes overemphasize age and "promotion" factors. Ollis, Macpherson, and Collins (2006) showed development pathways of officials don't always follow conventional stages, but rather are discontinuous and the outcome of an array of normative (i.e., transition points, training, prescribed learning materials) and non-normative influences (i.e., adverse game experiences, luck). Furthermore, the potential transfer of skills from other contexts (i.e., athlete experiences) stresses the need to consider the complete ecology of officials' developmental environment, including various interacting influences on developmental trajectory, such as inter-personal relationships, intra-personal characteristics, group characteristics, and cultural factors (Ollis et al., 2006).

We believe Newell's theoretical model of constraints (individual, environmental, and task) may be a useful tool in these regards (even if it is just a starting point). We feel that at this stage (particularly with respect to understanding the development of sport officials), a framework should be simultaneously comprehensive, parsimonious, and intuitive, and needs to explicitly accommodate the fact that officials, officiating tasks, and contexts are multidimensional and non-homogeneous. In many ways, this model incorporates elements of Plessner and MacMahon's (2013) taxonomy and of the Cornerstones model (Mascarenhas et al., 2005), while also expanding to include other important factors, most notably environmental characteristics.

A Constraints-Based Model of Officiating

Originally conceptualized to understand coordinated movement (see Haywood & Gretchell, 2014; Newell, 1986), Newell's model has since been used by others as a tool for organizing systematic reviews (Rienhoff et al., 2016; Webdale et al., 2019), as well as for understanding athlete development (Phillips, Davids, Renshaw, & Portus, 2010; Renshaw, Davids, Phillips, & Kerhervé, 2012; Wattie, Schorer, & Baker, 2015). This model proposes that outcomes are the result of interactions between three types of constraints: Individual, task, and environmental (see Figure 3.1). The nature of constraints is that they can have both positive and negative influences. Furthermore, it can sometimes be difficult to categorize variables into independent categories. As will become clear, distinguishing three independent categories is inherently difficult in a

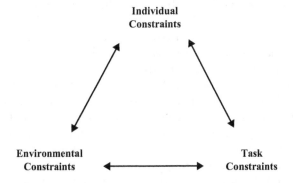

Figure 3.1 Depiction of Newell's model of constraints.

model explicitly based on interactions. Nevertheless, the importance of interactions highlights the need for an ecological approach. In the sections below, we attempt to rationalize the relevance of each constraint with respect to understanding officiating. We also try to emphasize the importance of interactions between constraints, and the directionality within the model.

Individual Constraints

Within this framework, individual constraints refer to the characteristics and capacities of the performer, in this case sport officials. There are two sub-categories of individual constraints: *Structural* and *functional*. Structural individual constraints refer to relatively stable factors such as height, weight, limb proportions, and sex. Functional individual constraints refer to factors such as fitness, strength, knowledge, perceptual-cognitive skill, and psychological characteristics.[1] These are often less stable and more adaptable. It is hard to argue that individual constraints are not important to include within a model of sport officiating. For example, in their recent integrative review of research on football referees, Pina and colleagues (Pina, Passos, Araújo, & Maynard, 2018) identified 7 research themes and 55 subthemes. Of the 55 subthemes, approximately 70% focused on individual structural or functional constraints, mostly within the areas of physical performance, technical performance, psychology, and physiology.

While there have been some studies on individual structural constraints in sport officials (see da Silva, Fernandez, Paes, Fernandes, & Rech, 2011), the history of officiating sport science is replete with studies of individual functional constraints. These studies have included a range of functional constraints, including personality type/characteristics (Alker, Straub, & Leary, 1973; Fratzke, 1975), measures of stress and coping skills (Louvet, Gaudreau, Menaut, Genty, & Deneuve, 2009; Voight, 2009), communication skills (Cunningham, Simmons, Mascarenhas, & Redhead, 2014), officiating self-efficacy (Guillén & Feltz, 2011), perceptual-cognitive skills (e.g., Helsen & Bultynck, 2004; Pizzera, 2015), motivation to engage in officiating and to cease officiating (Auger, Fortier, Thibault, Magny, & Gravelle, 2010; Hancock, Dawson, & Auger, 2015). Both structural and functional constraints are also encapsulated in occurrences of injury among football referees, and the subsequent influence on participation and performance (Bizzini, Junge, Bahr, & Dvorak, 2011; Wilson, Byrne, & Gissane, 2011). Individual functional constraints are also the point of emphasis in the Cornerstones Model of Refereeing Performance (i.e., knowledge, judgment, personality, game management, fitness, technique, and positions: Mascarenhas et al., 2005). Importantly, all of these constraints can influence a range of outcomes, including participation, retention, and performance during competition, and they distinguish skilled from less skilled officials.

Although individual constraints in and of themselves are a tremendously important element of the sport science on officials, it is also important to consider their *interaction* with other constraints. The role of sex and/or gender illustrates this point nicely. Although underrepresented in officiating research (Pina et al., 2018), female officials can have markedly different experiences than male officials (see Forbes, Edwards, & Fleming, 2015; Tingle, Warner, & Sartore-Baldwin, 2014). Not only do female officials experience sexism and marginalization, but they also often have to negotiate their identities as females and develop a range of inter/intra-personal strategies to overcome barriers and conflict. As such, understanding the different experiences and opportunities for female versus male officials requires an acknowledgement of environmental constraints (i.e., sexism and homophobia) in broader society as well as the culture of sport (Fink, 2016; Jones & Edwards, 2013). In summary, the interaction between an individual constraints (e.g., sex and/or gender) and environmental constraints (e.g., sexism) can not only influence retention, participation, and performance, but may also influence the development of self-efficacy, motivation, and other social skills.

Task Constraints

In this context, task constraints refer to the demands of officiating in a specific sport, which can also vary based on unique roles within a sport (e.g., central match official(s) versus linesmen/assistants; see Catteeuw, Helsen, Gilis, & Wagemans, 2009; Wilson, Bynre, & Gissane, 2011). These demands can, and do, differ significantly by sport and role. They can differ based on knowledge (e.g., number and complexity of rules), physical, perceptual-cognitive complexity, and communication demands. Moreover, these demands can differ *within* a sport, based on the skill level of the athletes. The importance of considering the variation in officiating demands has certainly been a point of focus for researchers. As described earlier, Plessner and MacMahon (2013) describe the task constraints of officiating based on the number of cues and/or athletes that have to be monitored, the amount of interaction and/or movement involved, and the psychological demands involved while officiating.

Based on the degrees of these three factors, they classified officials and their demands as *interactors, monitors,* and *reactors* (for more discussion on this model and task constraints, see Chapter 5). Interactors have to attend to a heightened number of cues, and are typically more physically involved in the action of the game (e.g., basketball and soccer referees). Monitors typically have moderate to low physical demands and interaction with athletes, but still have a large number of cues to keep track of while officiating (e.g., volleyball referees). Last, reactors deal with the fewest number of cues and are the least interactively engaged with athletes (i.e., judges and umpires). However, reactors' judgments might be considered by some to be at the lower end of the continuum in terms of demands and complexity; it is important to note their judgments are often in the context of significant time constraints. What this framework makes clear is that officiating, even within a category, is incredibly heterogeneous.

While the taxonomy by Plessner and MacMahon (2013) provides a useful way to conceptualize the diversity of officiating demands, there are also elements of officiating that are not captured by this framework. More difficult to quantify and describe is the degree of discretion afforded to officials. Livingston and Forbes' (2003) content analysis of international rulebooks found that soccer and basketball officials are more empowered than hockey officials (based on the language used in rule manuals). Major League Baseball umpires also certainly have a reputation for having bespoke strike zones. As such, while all officials must enforce the rules of the game and/or judge performance, the extent to which officials have discretion and control over the game may depend upon the sport (in some cases understanding discretion in the development of sport officials requires a socio-historical lens: See Webb, 2014).

It will also be important to explore the malleability of task constraints. For example, rules and styles of play can change over time, which can influence the demands placed on officials. Informed models of officiating development will require a detailed understanding of how task (as well as individual and environment) constraints change at different levels of expertise (i.e., novice, intermediate, advanced, elite; Baker, Schorer, & Wattie, 2015). Increasingly, the task of officiating is also demanding the use of technology to augment the arbitration of sporting contests (e.g., video reply; video assistant referees).

Environmental Constraints

Environmental constraints generally describe factors that are more dynamic and outside the demands of a task. At the outset, it is important to acknowledge that environmental constraints can be difficult to distinguish from task constraints, and in some circumstances, individual constraints. For example, consider a football official refereeing an outdoor match, in cold weather, with persistent fine rain (i.e., a typical and delightful British day). Is the weather an environmental constraint or a task constraint? Similarly, perceived organizational support (see Livingston & Forbes, 2016, 2017) can be interpreted as an indicator of an environmental constraint (the characteristics of sport/officiating organizations) and/or an individual constraint (the *perception* of one's environment). Ultimately, to decide whether to classify constraints as sport or as environmentally derived, we chose here to rely on a simple heuristic: *Could that constraint in question change from day to day, or place-to-place?* If a constraint was not fundamental to the task at hand (i.e., a common element from contest to contest), we chose to describe such factors as environmental constraints.

Environmental constraints may also arguably be the most diverse category. This category can include factors such as the natural environment (e.g., climate and geography), the built environment (e.g., roads and infrastructure of stadiums or venues), inter-personal relations (e.g., relationships and interactions with other officials, sport organizations, family and friends), organizational programs and resources, and the broader context of a competition (e.g., rival sectarian teams, or elimination versus regular league game). This category of constraints also includes factors such as sociocultural norms and values, as well as social policies.

We believe that understanding processes and outcomes related to sport officiating requires an appreciation for the influence of environmental factors. Any model that seeks to understand developmental outcomes for sport officials needs to understand the environmental factors. Indeed, research on optimal athlete development environments (see Henriksen & Stambulova, 2017; Slack et al., 2013) reinforces the importance that a range of outcomes are influenced by multiple environmental characteristics.

The inclusion of environmental factors within a framework for studying officials is not a controversial one. There are many examples in the officiating literature that illustrate the interaction between environmental, task, and individual constraints (in particular the performance of individual functional constraints: Perceptual-cognitive skill). For example, environmental factors such as crowds (e.g., noise, size, proximity to competition area: Balmer et al., 2007; Downward & Jones, 2007; Nevill, Balmer, & Williams, 2002; Unkelbach & Memmert, 2010) and the home team (e.g., Balmer, Nevill, & Lane, 2005; Johnston, 2008; Nevill & Holder, 1999) can influence (bias) officials' decisions (individual functional constraint). Even the color of players' attire can influence the judgments of sport officials (Hagemann, Strauss, & Leißing, 2008). Strictly speaking, these environmental factors do not alter the task demands per se, though they do interact with individual's perceptual-cognitive skill (individual functional constraints) to influence performance.

Implications for Research and Practice

Adopting this ecological framework has a number of benefits and implications. One of the benefits of adopting a framework that incorporates multiple constraints is that findings take on a higher degree of ecological validity. Naturally, it can require added effort to collect additional measure, or compare multiple groups. However, the research on athlete development demonstrates the promise of holistic ecological approaches to the development of athletes (see Henriksen & Stambulova, 2017). We believe that the same is true of sport officials.

One of the implications of a framework that emphasizes the fact that outcomes are the result of interactions between multiple constraints is that the unit of measurement becomes the interaction: Individual-task, individual-environment, task-environment, or individual-task-environment. As such, the emphasis may not be on a single dependent measures per se, but the interaction term itself. In doing so, it is important to purposefully measure variables. Comparative designs can be useful in these approaches, as they provide an opportunity to compare the influence of variations in certain constraints (e.g., comparing officials from the same sport, but in different cultural or organizational contexts).

With respect to developmental outcomes and processes, Wattie and colleagues (2015) have suggested that there are two useful research approaches to using this framework: *Macro and micro approaches.* Macro approaches take a broad focus and comprehensively measure multiple constraints, seeking to better understand the unique variance of specific constraints and salient interactions between constraints. This approach attempts to be as ecologically valid as possible. Alternatively, this framework also permits micro approaches to research. This approach entails focusing on a smaller number of specific constraints, perhaps in experimental designs. For example, when one constraint is manipulated or changed, the impact on another constraint(s) can be measured. This could be done in experimental lab studies or in natural experiments such as when an organization alters the resources and support for sport officials (environmental constraints: Arguably, the studies on crowd noise and size are examples of micro approaches to studies on sport officials). As a result, this model can also be used to generate and test hypotheses (Wattie et al., 2015).

As others have done (Reinhoff et al., 2018; Webdale et al., 2019), this theoretical framework can be used to quantify the state of science on officiating through systematic and integrative reviews. *Are there imbalances in what is known, or not known, about the role of specific constraints? Have specific constraints been explored in some sports, but not others?* Using an approach proposed by Wattie and colleagues (2015), researchers could quantify and visually depict the state of sport science in this area. We provide a first level to this by presenting an illustration of where officiating study topics fit within a multiple constraints model (see Figure 3.2). In a more advanced analysis, the proportion or absolute number of studies that examine specific constraints could be depicted as pie pieces for each constraint. In addition, using multivariate (macro) approaches, a newer model that tabulates study proportions could also be used to represent the unique (and shared) variance explained by constraints. In this case, the size of the pie pieces could be standardized using variance measures, effect size metrics, or likelihood estimates.

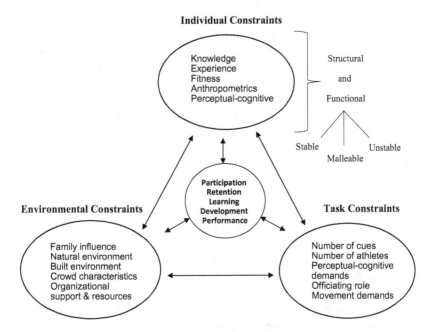

Figure 3.2 Example depiction of officiating study for constraints.

This framework can also be used as a more applied tool or thought exercise for practitioners. For example, practitioners could itemize and depict the individual, task, and environmental constraints that need to be taken into account when designing and implementing a sport-specific development program for officials. They could even create stage-specific (i.e., age and performance level) summaries and plans of the constraints that exist at different stages in officiating development. The framework also aligns with promising pedagogical approaches, such as the constraints-led approach (Chow, Davids, Button, & Renshaw, 2016; Renshaw, Davids, & Savelsberg, 2010). With an understanding of the relevant constraints for a specific sport context, educators and officials could attempt to manipulate relevant constraints when designing learning opportunities and training resources.

Summary

It is important to reiterate that we view this theoretical framework and model as a starting point: A new way forward and way to help better conceptualize officiating experiences, demands, and participation. As a model of interpretation, it provides a basis to evaluate existing research, inform research future, and guide practitioners. It is possible that existing theories, or elements of theories, will prove appropriate to explain processes and outcomes. For example, MacMahon and colleagues (2015) suggested that the FTEM model could also apply to the development of sport officials based on differing participation, professionalization, and career pathways of officials (see Chapter 7 for further discussion about the FTEM model). This model may indeed prove to be a well-suited developmental model for sport officials; however, our aim in proposing a constraints-based framework for understanding officials, and officiating, is to advocate for holistic and comprehensive approaches to the study and development of sport officials. We believe whatever model ultimately emerges as predominant, that it will be compromised, and ecologically invalid, if it considers officials and officiating outcomes divorced from relevant task, individual, *and* environment constraints.

TAKE AWAY MESSAGES FROM THIS CHAPTER

- It is important to have a guiding framework (or theory) to understand the spectrum of factors that influence the development and performance of sport officials.
- Current models of sport officiating are often performance- or skill-based and categorize officials based on their task complexity. Such models might not explicitly account for other compounding factors that influence officials' performance and learning.
- Integrating ecological perspectives into understanding officials, and officiating, raises consideration to other impinging factors, processes, and tensions that surround and influence officials' activity, participation, performance, and development.

CONSTRAINTS MODEL OF SPORT OFFICIATING

- *Individual constraints* can be more structural or fixed in nature, while others more functional and adaptive. Such constraints that differ official-to-official are also more stable (height, personality), unstable (change day-to-day), and malleable.
- Officials' sport and sport-role predict the unique constraints that define their task demands. Such *task constraints* can differ based on knowledge (e.g., number and complexity of rules), physical, perceptual-cognitive complexity, and communication demands.

- Acknowledgement of the range of *environmental constraints* that influence officials is imperative. This can include physical or natural (e.g., indoor or outdoor or large versus small venues), sociocultural (e.g., larger sport community), interpersonal (e.g., relationships and interactions with other officials, sport organizations, family and friends), and organizational environment provided by officiating development programs, resources, and supports.
- The implication of an ecologically based constraints model allows for micro and macro approaches to study interactions among constraints. From a practical perspective, by accounting for individual, task, and environmental influences on your sport-specific officials' participation and performance, representative officiating development plans (ODP; see Chapter 7) can be greatly informed and developed.

Note

1 In Chapter 4, we elaborate on these constraints based on Dehghansai and colleague's (Dehghansai, Lemez, Wattie, Baker, & Pinder, under review) suggestion to specify functional constraints as either stable, malleable, or unstable.

References

Alker, H.A., Straub, W.F., & Leary, J. (1973). Achieving consistency: A study of basketball officiating. *Journal of Vocational Behavior, 3,* 335–343.

Auger, D., Fortier, J., Thibault, A., Magny, D., & Gravelle, F. (2010). Characteristics and motivations of sports officials in the province of Québec. *International Journal of Sport Management, Recreation & Tourism, 5,* 29–50.

Baker, J., & Wattie, N. (in press). Athlete development models. In D. Gould & C. Mallett (Eds.), *The sports coaching handbook.* Champaign, IL: Human Kinetics.

Balmer, N.J., Nevill, A.M., & Lane, A.M. (2005). Do judges enhance home advantage in European championship boxing? *Journal of Sports Sciences, 23,* 409–416.

Balmer, N.J., Nevill, A.M., Lane, A.M., Ward, P., Williams, A. M., & Fairclough, S.H. (2007). Influence of crowd noise on soccer refereeing consistency in soccer. *Journal of Sport Behavior, 30,* 130–145.

Bizzini, M., Junge, A., Bahr, R., & Dvorak, J. (2011). Injuries of football referees: A representative survey of Swiss referees officiating at all levels of play. *Scandinavian Journal of Medicine and Science in Sports, 21,* 42–47.

Catteeuw, P., Helsen, W. F., Gilis, B., & Wagemans, J. (2009). Decision-making skills, role specificity, and deliberate practice in association football refereeing. *Journal of Sports Sciences, 27,* 1125–1136. doi:10.1080/02640410903079179

Chow, J.Y., Davids, K., Button, C., & Renshaw, I. (2016). *Nonlinear pedagogy in skill acquisition: An introduction.* London: Routledge.

Côté, J., Baker, J., & Abernethy, B. (2007). Practice and play in the development of sport expertise. In R. Eklund & G. Tenenbaum (Eds.), *Handbook of sport psychology* (3rd ed., pp. 184–202). Hoboken, NJ: Wiley.

Côté, J., & Fraser-Thomas, J. (2016). Youth involvement and positive development in sport. In P.R.E. Crocker (Ed.), *Sport and exercise psychology: A Canadian perspective* (pp. 256–287). Toronto: Pearson.

Cunningham, I., Mascarenhas, D., Simmons, P., & Rix-Lièvre, G. (under review). Team captains' activity during actual interactions with sport officials. *Psychology of Sport and Exercise.*

Cunningham, I., Simmons, P., Mascarenhas, D., & Redhead, S. (2014). Concepts of communication and player management in the development of sport officials. *International Journal of Sport Communication, 7*, 166–187.

Dehghansai, N., Lemez, S., Wattie, N., & Baker, J. (under review). Understanding the development of elite parasport athletes: Current understanding and future directions. *International Journal of Sports Science & Coaching.*

Downward, P., & Jones, M. (2007). Effects of crowd size on referee decisions: Analysis of the FA Cup. *Journal of Sports Sciences, 25*, 1541–1545.

Fink, J. (2016). Hiding in plain sight: The embedded nature of sexism in sport. *Journal of Sport Management, 30*, 1–7.

Forbes, A., Edwards, L., & Fleming, S. (2015). 'Women can't referee': Exploring the experiences of female football officials within UK football culture. *Soccer & Society, 16*, 521–539.

Fratzke, M.R. (1975). Personality and biographical traits of superior and average college basketball officials. *The Research Quarterly, 46*, 484–488.

Green, C. (2005). Building sport programs to optimize athlete recruitment, retention, and transition: Toward a normative theory of sport development. *Journal of Sport Management, 19*, 233–253.

Gulbin, J.P., Croser, M.J., Morley, E.J., & Weissensteiner, J.R. (2013). An integrated framework for the optimisation of sport and athlete development: A practitioner approach. *Journal of Sports Sciences, 31*, 1319–1331.

Güllich, A. (2019). "Macro-structure" of developmental participation histories and "micro-structure" of practice in German female world-class and national-class football players. *Journal of Sport Sciences, 37*, 1347–1355.

Hagemann, N., Strauss, B., & Leißing, J. (2008). When the referee sees red ... *Psychological Science, 19*, 769–771.

Hancock, D.J., Dawson, D.J., & Auger, D. (2015). Why ref? Understanding sports officials' motivations to begin, continue, and quit. *Movement & Sport Sciences, 87*, 31–39.

Haywood, K., & Getchell, N. (2014). Fundamental Concepts. In *Life Span Motor Development* (6th ed., pp. 3–15). Champaign, IL: Human Kinetics.

Helsen, W., & Bultynck, J.B. (2004). Physical and perceptual-cognitive demands of top-class refereeing in association football. *Journal of Sports Sciences, 22*, 179–189.

Henriksen, K., & Stambulova, N. (2017). Creating optimal environments for talent development: A holistic ecological approach. In J. Baker, S. Cobley, J. Schorer, & N. Wattie (Eds), *The Routledge Handbook of Talent Identification and Development in Sport.* London: Routledge.

Jones, C., & Edwards, L.L. (2013). The woman in black: Exposing sexist beliefs about female officials in elite men's football. *Sport, Ethics and Philosophy, 7*, 202–216.

Lewin, K. (1951). *Field theory in social science.* New York: Harper & Brothers.

Livingston, L.A., & Forbes, S.L. (2003). Rule modification and strict rule enforcement as a means of reducing injury in invasion games? *Avante, 8,* 12–20.

Livingston, L.A., & Forbes, S.L. (2016). Factors contributing to the retention of Canadian amateur sport officials: Motivations, perceived organizational support, and resilience. *International Journal of Sports Science & Coaching, 11*(3), 342–355.

Livingston, L.A., & Forbes, S.L. (2017). Resilience, motivations for participation, and perceived organizational support amongst aesthetic sports officials. *Journal of Sport Behavior, 40*(1), 43–67.

Livingston, L.A., Forbes, S.L., Pearson, N., Camacho, T., Wattie, N., & Varian, P. (2017). Sport officiating recruitment, development, and retention: A call to action. *Current Issues in Sport Science, 2,* 011. doi: 10.15203/CISS_2017.011

Louvet, B., Gaudreau, P., Menaut, A., Genty, J., & Deneuve, P. (2009). Revisiting the changing and stable properties of coping utilization using latent class growth analysis: a longitudinal investigation with soccer referees. *Psychology of Sport and Exercise, 10,* 124–135.

MacMahon, C., Helsen, W.F., Starkes, J.L., & Weston, M. (2007). Decision-making skills and deliberate practice in elite association football referees. *Journal of Sports Sciences, 25*(1), 65–78.

MacMahon, C., Mascarenhas, D., Plessner, H., Pizzera, A., Oudejans, R., & Raab, M. (2015). Development of sports officials. In *Sports officials and officiating: Science and Practice* (pp. 8–32). London: Routledge.

Mascarenhas, D.R.D., Collins, D., & Mortimer, P. (2005). Elite refereeing performance: developing a model for sport science support. *The Sport Psychologist, 19,* 364–379.

Nevill, A.M., Balmer, N.J., & Williams, A.M. (1999). Crowd influence on decisions in association football. *The Lancet, 353,* 1416–1416.

Nevill, A.M., Balmer, N.J., & Williams, A.M. (2002). The influence of crowd noise and experience upon refereeing decisions in football. *Psychology of Sport and Exercise, 3,* 261–272.

Nevill, A.M., & Holder, R.L. (1999). Home advantage in sport: an overview of studies on the advantage of playing at home. *Sports Medicine, 28,* 221–236.

Newell, K.M. (1986). Constraints on the development of coordination. In M.G. Wade & H.T.A. Whiting (Eds.), *Motor development in children: Aspects of coordination and control* (pp. 341–361). Amsterdam, The Netherlands: Martin Nijhoff.

Ollis, S., Macpherson, A., & Collins, D. (2006). Expertise and talent development in rugby refereeing: An ethnographic enquiry. *Journal of Sports Sciences, 24,* 309–322.

Phillips, E., Davids, K., Renshaw, I., & Portus, M. (2010). Expert performance in sports and the dynamics of talent development. *Sports Medicine, 40,* 1–13.

Pina, J.A., Passos, A., Araújo, D., & Maynard, M.T. (2018). Football refereeing: An integrative review. *Psychology of Sport & Exercise, 35,* 10–26.

Pizzera, A. (2015). The role of embodied cognition in sports officiating. *Movement & Sport Sciences, 87,* 53–61.

Plessner, H., & MacMahon, C. (2013). The sport official in research and practice. In D. Farrow, J. Baker, & C. MacMahon (Eds.), *Developing sport expertise: Researchers and coaches put theory into practice* (2nd ed., pp. 71–95). London: Routledge.

Renshaw, I., Davids, K., Phillips, E., & Kerhervé, H. (2012). Developing talent in athletes as complex neurobiological systems. In J. Baker, S. Cobley, & J. Schorer (Eds.), *Talent identification and development in sport: International perspectives* (pp. 64–80). London: Routledge.

Renshaw, I., Davids, K., & Savelsberg, G.J.P. (2010). *Motor learning in practice: A constraints-led approach*. London: Routledge.

Rienhoff, R., Tirp, J., Strauß, B., Baker, J., & Schorer, J. (2016). The 'quiet eye' and motor performance: A systematic review based on Newell's constraints-led model. *Sports Medicine, 46,* 589–603.

Rix-Lièvre, G., Boyer, S., Terfous, F., Coutarel, F., & Lièvre, P. (2015). La co-production de la performance arbitrale de haut niveau: le case du rugby. *Sociologie du Travail, 57,* 496–515.

Russell, S., Renshaw, I., & Davids, K. (2019). How interacting constraints shape emergent decision-making of national-level football referees. *Qualitative Research in Sport, Exercise and Health, 11,* 573–588.

da Silva, A. I., Fernandez, R., Paes, M. R., Fernandes, L. C., & Rech, C. R. (2011). Somatotype and body composition of Brazilian football (soccer) referees. *Archivos de Medicina Del Deporte, 28,* 238–246.

Slack, L., Maynard, I., Butt, J., & Olusoga, P. (2013). Factors underpinning football officiating excellence: Perceptions of English premier league referees. *Journal of Applied Sport Psychology, 25,* 298–315.

Tingle, J.K., Warner, S., & Sartore-Baldwin, M.L. (2014). The experience of former women officials and the impact of the sporting community. *Sex Roles, 71,* 7–20.

Unkelbach, C., & Memmert, D. (2010). Crowd noise as a cue in referee decisions contributes to the home advantage. *Journal of Sport & Exercise Psychology, 32,* 483–498.

Voight, M. (2009). Sources of stress and coping strategies of US soccer officials. *Stress and Health, 25,* 91–101.

Wattie, N., Schorer, J., & Baker J. (2015). The relative age effect in sport: A developmental systems model. *Sports Medicine, 45,* 83–94.

Webb, T. (2014). The emergence of training and assessment for referees in association football: Moving from the side-lines. *The International Journal of the History of Sport, 31,* 1081–1097.

Webdale, K., Baker, J., Schorer, J., & Wattie, N. (2019). Solving sport's 'relative age' problem: A systematic review of proposed solutions. *International Review of Sport and Exercise Psychology.* doi:10.1080/1750984X.2019.1675083

Wilson, F., Byrne, A., & Gissane, C. (2011). A prospective study of injury and activity profile in elite soccer referees and assistant referees. *Irish Medical Journal, 104,* 295–297.

4 Individual Variation among Sport Officials
Categorizing Skills, Abilities, and Characteristics

The history of research on officiating has been dominated by an emphasis on the individual (see Pina, Passos, Araújo, & Maynard, 2018). The topics of these investigations include the physical, psychological, and perceptual-cognitive skills and characteristics of sport officials. In many respects, Mascarenhas, Collins, and Mortimer's (2005) Cornerstones Performance Model of Refereeing excellently describes the skills, abilities, and traits that dictate officials' performance (and therefore areas to target for developmental support). However, the framework we described in Chapter 3 proposes that there is some usefulness in also classifying individual characteristics into structural and functional categories. Structural characteristics refer predominantly to anthropometric and physiological structural differences between individuals (e.g., height, weight, muscle mass). Functional characteristics are more modifiable factors such as fitness, strength, knowledge, perceptual-cognitive skill, and certain psychological characteristics. For the most part, the Cornerstones model describes functional characteristics that are the constituent components necessary for successful officiating performance (i.e., knowledge and rules, contextual judgment, game management skills, and fitness, positioning, and mechanics).

Conceptualizing Variation in Sport Officials' Characteristics

The purpose of this chapter is to highlight the variation of individual characteristics (structural and functional; Newell, 1986) that influence the development and performance of sport officials, and also to highlight some important future direction for the study of sport officials. Based on the suggestions of Dehghansai and colleagues (under review), we believe that it may be useful to further consider these individual characteristics as *stable, malleable,* and *unstable.* This added distinction classifies structural and functional constraints based on their modifiability and predictability (see Table 4.1).

By considering these distinctions, officials and practitioners may be better able to structure training environments and activities and

Table 4.1 Individual characteristics that influence the performance and development capacity

Type of Constraint	Characteristics	Examples
Structural Constraints		
Stable	Body structures that are relatively stable over time	Height
Malleable	Body structures that adapt long-term to task demands and training	Muscle mass
Unstable	Body structures that are transient and changes are relatively unpredictable	Musculoskeletal injuries
Functional Constraints		
Stable	Psychological, cognitive, and behavioral characteristics that are relatively stable over time	Personality
Malleable	Psychological, cognitive, and behavioral characteristics that are modifiable	Self-efficacy and perceptual-cognitive skill
Unstable	Affective, cognitive, and behavioral states that are transient and can change day-to-day	Mood and mental fatigue

understand the influence of inter-individual variation in skills and abilities on officiating talent and expertise development. Ultimately, we propose that knowing whether officials' characteristics, skills, and abilities are *stable, malleable,* or *unstable* can equip researchers and practitioners to better optimize the recruitment and development of officials. For the practitioner, it can aid to characterize officials' development needs and strengths, anticipate trajectories, and explain factors that shape performance processes and outcomes. For the officiating researchers, this categorization provides a model for explaining other unstudied individual factors influencing officials' performance and skill development and for interpreting pre-existing empirical research in the officiating field. We expand on these classifications in the following sections and discuss their implications for the performance and development of sport officials.

Stable Structural Constraints

As the title implies, stable structural constraints are those that are relatively fixed and unchangeable (or that change slowly with age). Examples include characteristics such as height, limb length, and innate aerobic capacity. With some exceptions, stable structural constraints have not been extensively studied in officiating populations (see Pina et al., 2018), though there are indications and these characteristics may influence performance and development.

In sports where the physical demands of officiating are high, stable structural characteristics, such as aerobic capacity, can play an important role. For example, aerobic fitness has been directly related to officiating performance in soccer (see Castagna, Abt, & D'Ottavio, 2007). Certainly, structural physiology related to aerobic capacity is trainable (see Malleable Structural Constraints). However, there are structural limits for such capacities (i.e., strength, aerobic capacity, and responsiveness to training) as a result of genetic limits (Bouchard et al., 1998; Bouchard et al., 1999; Calvo et al., 2002; Rankinen et al., 2006). Ultimately, these limits may constrain how much a change can come about through training, and therefore the future potential of officials.

Anthropometric characteristics are also stable, and relatively fixed. Estimates suggest that approximately 80% of height is explained by genetic factors, and therefore fairly stable (McEvoy & Visscher, 2009). Characteristics like anthropometrics can affect performance through their influence on a myriad of variables that need to be optimally coordinated in order to attain a given performance outcome. For example, differences in height and/or limb length may provide referees and judges with different action opportunities (i.e., affordances – see Araújo & Davids, 2009). These characteristics may also influence cognitive judgments and decision-making. Pizzera (2015) argues that officials' performance reflects embodied cognition, wherein cognitive judgments are linked to individuals' motor and visual (perceptual) experiences. For example, *could the height of a line judge in tennis (i.e., their vantage point) influence their perception of where balls land, and consequently the accuracy of their judgments? Could a soccer match central official's limb length influence their movement patterns and ability to arrive in an optimal position for an accurate viewing angle of match play?*

To our knowledge, talent identification as a discipline in sport science (see Baker, Cobley, & Schorer, 2012; Baker, Cobley, Schorer, & Wattie, 2017) has not been extensively applied to sport officials. While stable structural constraints, like anthropometrics, have been extensively studied for talent identification and development of athletes (see Norton & Olds, 2001; Robinson, Wattie, Schorer, & Baker, 2018), to our knowledge there has been little-to-no attention to these characteristics from a talent identification or development perspective among officials. *Is there an optimal alignment between structural characteristics and specific officiating roles/sports?* In sports, athletes' bodies have become increasingly specialized and sport-specific to reflect bodies that have task-specific performance advantages (see "expanding universe of athletic bodies": p. 763, Norton & Olds, 2001). It may be worth considering if a similar specialization of structural characteristics is occurring and/or would benefit officials in certain roles.

While some stable structural characteristics may not directly influence performance and development, they may also interact with environmental factors (i.e., inter-personal communication and evaluations) in important ways. For example, depending on the sport, characteristics such as age, height, weight, aesthetics, and sex/gender may serve as cues that influence impressions and perceptions of officials' fairness and competence (Dosseville, Laborde, & Bernier, 2014; Simmons, 2011). Some suggestions indicate that earlier recruitment and/or 'fast-tracking' of officials may be influenced by perceptions of officials' youthfulness, athleticism, and how presentable they are for television (Sharpe, Synnott, Cunningham, & Ordway, 2019). Similarly, the unique experiences that female officials have interacting with players, coaches, and spectators (Forbes, Edwards, & Fleming, 2015; Tingle, Warner, & Sartore-Baldwin, 2014), as well as the subsequent inter-personal skills and strategies they must develop, suggest that stable characteristics are salient influences on the development of sport officials. While biases are frequently mentioned within athlete talent identification and development processes (Abbott, Button, Pepping, & Collins, 2005; Baker, Schorer, & Wattie, 2018; Koz, Fraser-Thomas, & Baker, 2012; Robinson et al., 2018; Wattie & Baker, 2018), this topic has not been significantly discussed for sport officials. The collective examples discussed above suggest that perceptions of officials' performance may be influenced by stable structural characteristics such as anthropometrics and appearance.

Malleable Structural Constraints

Malleable structural constraints refer to body structures that adapt to the demands of a task, primarily due to long-term engagement in officiating and/or training (Newell, Liu, & Mayer-Kress, 2001; Newell, Mayer-Kress, Hong, & Liu, 2009, 2010). Examples include gains in muscle mass, changes to vasculature, and changes to neural pathways. What is clear is that the sport-specific demands of officiating necessitate training and adaptation to facilitate performance, and that without sufficient training development across the officiating ranks may be highly constrained. Arguably, the most emphasized malleable structural characteristics relate to speed and aerobic fitness. Sports such as soccer, rugby, ice hockey, basketball, and American football all necessitate varying levels of speed and aerobic endurance. Moreover, the demands within each sport vary depending on the age and expertise level of the athletes that are being refereed.

As the development of sport officials garners more attention and resources, it will be important to consider specific types of training and consider how this may impede or facilitate performance and development (see Castagna et al., 2007). For example, we have heard anecdotal reports that some soccer referees continue to play soccer as athletes partly as a means of training and maintaining fitness levels necessary to support refereeing performance. As the development of officials becomes more structured and supported by sport organizations, it may also be necessary to consider the predispositions and innate capacities of individuals when creating individual performance and training plans, and making decisions about officials' future potential.

Unstable Structural Constraints

In contrast to stable and malleable structural constraints, unstable constraints are more unpredictable, and generally not a purposeful goal or desired outcome of training, but that nonetheless involve changes anthropometric and physiological bodily structures. For example, while there can be improvements in performance as a result of structural changes due to training session and competition, there may also be variation in performance due to changes in bodily structures. These characteristics are 'unstable' because they can vary day-to-day. Perhaps, the most salient example for many officials may be factors such as stiffness, soreness, and/or injury (Gabrilo et al., 2013). Research on injuries among sport officials has primarily focused on prevalence and context. Research on soccer referees suggests that injuries are much more likely to occur during training and fitness assessment tests, rather than during games (e.g., Bizzini, Junge, Bahr, & Dvorak, 2011; Oliveira, Reis, & Inácio, 2016). Overall, research suggests that injuries are common, predominantly minor (sprains and strains), reflect officials' age, and task demands of officiating that sport (i.e., Achilles and hamstring injuries in a soccer refereeing context: Bizzini, Junge, Bahr, & Dvorak, 2009, 2011). Compared to athletes, however, there is much that we do not know about the influence of injuries on officials' development and performance. For example, it is not clear how common it is for officials to officiate while injured, and what influence injury has on the quality of officials' judgments. Furthermore, given that many officials have a history of participation as an athlete, it is not clear what, if any, the influence is of injuries sustained prior to officiating.[1]

For sport organizations, it appears to be very important to consider for officials: (i) The quality of training programs and guidelines provided to them and (ii) the risk of injury and impact of fitness tests on their health and well-being. Given the relatively minor nature of many injuries (sprains and strains), it is important for evaluators and supervisors to view injuries as minor constraints on performance and development, and not to let perceptions of injuries limit officials' opportunities for development. In sports that warrant it, there also needs to be systems in place to support injured officials, and potentially to have 'return to play' protocols in place.

Stable Functional Constraints

Stable functional constraints describe characteristics, such as psychological traits, which generally do not change over time. These characteristics may be more accurately assessed independent of variables (e.g., decision-making skill) related to accumulated training, amount of experience, and availability of instructional resources (Baker, Schorer, & Wattie, 2019). For example, some measures of personality[2] that underpin skill and performance are more stable over time (Penke, Denissen, & Miller, 2007). Indeed, one of the earliest points of interest in the officiating sport science literature was officials' personality types (see Alker, Straub, & Leary, 1973; Fratzke, 1975; Ittenbach & Eller, 1989). There are indications that personality types (e.g., high levels of conscientiousness: Duty, persistence, self-disciplined goal-directed behavior, organized, responsible, and efficient; Pervin, Cervone, & John, 2005) correlate positively with quality ratings of officials' judgments (Sayfollahpour, Ganjooee, & Nikbakhsh, 2013).

Going forward, it will be important to consider *how* personality is used to guide officiating development programs. While an official's increased awareness about their personality traits can help them better manage these attributes during performance (Cunningham et al., 2014), it may be important to consider biases in formally appraising stable functional characteristics like personality. Evidence suggests that athletes and fans may have inaccurate or biased view of officials' personality characteristics, perceiving them as more neurotic, less extraverted, and less agreeable as a group (Balch & Scott, 2007). This reinforces the need for objective assessment methods of assessing officials' personality types when recruiting, developing, and evaluating sport officials. Furthermore, Baker et al. (2019) suggest that stable factors like personality type may have moderating or mediating influences (Barron & Kenny, 1986)[3] on development and expertise attainment. Specifically, there are indicators that personality (e.g., conscientiousness, Bergeman et al., 1993; selfishness, ruthlessness, Hardy et al., 2017; perfectionism, Smith et al., 2019) may influence the relationship between training behaviors (e.g., inclination and motivation to practice) and attainment level. Therefore, it may be necessary to consider how variations in personality profiles are related to different experiences during training and competition, and the subsequent influence on attainment. Furthermore, it may be useful to consider if/how personality influences cohesion among groups of officials when they must work in teams/crews (see Aeron & Pathak, 2012; Hancock, Martin, Paradis, & Evans, 2018), such as in basketball, soccer, and ice hockey.

Malleable Functional Constraints

Within the classification of malleable functional constraints are internal characteristics that are more variable over time and more malleable to changes. These factors affect performance and development (e.g., Glazier & Robins, 2013). A number of these characteristics are described by Mascarenhas and colleagues (2005) in their Cornerstones Model of Refereeing Performance. These include, but are not limited to, internal factors such as knowledge, motivation, inter-personal skills, and self-efficacy. While this category can include many different skills and characteristics, we include only a selection below to illustrate the concept and relevance to officiating performance and development.

Self-Efficacy

Self-efficacy refers to an individual's judgments of their capabilities to successfully organize and execute courses of action to produce specific outcomes (Bandura, 1997). This psychological characteristic is highly domain specific, and it is a robust predictor of motivation, current behavior, effort, resilience to failure, emotional control, as well as future behaviors and performance (Bandura, 1997; Feltz, Short, & Sullivan, 2008). Importantly, people with higher self-efficacy are more likely to respond to adversity by increasing their efforts to improve performance (Maddux, 1995). Self-efficacy for officiating reflects confidence in the skills and abilities that are needed for effective performance. Specifically, the proposed dimensions of officiating self-efficacy (in team invasion, ball sports) include game knowledge, decision-making, coping with pressure/stress, communication (Myers et al., 2012), and fitness and positioning (Guillén & Feltz, 2011; Lirgg, Feltz, & Merrie, 2016). Officials with higher levels of officiating-specific self-efficacy are suggested to be more satisfied and committed in their role, feel less stress, make faster and more consistently accurate decisions (Guillén & Feltz, 2011; Lirgg et al., 2016).

There is a need to understand how changes in self-efficacy influence development and performance (Livingston et al., 2017). There is also a need for sport organizations and developmental programs to explicitly design ways to increase self-efficacy among officials (i.e., through past performance, vicarious experience, physiological/affective experiences, and social persuasion; Myers et al., 2012), particularly during the entry-level stages of participation. Indeed, additional research on the *sources* of officiating self-efficacy may provide some insight into the benefits of prior participation as an athlete (e.g., there may be some important transfer of self-efficacy for game knowledge). Mastery experiences (i.e., years spent officiating) is frequently shown to predict greater self-efficacy in officials (Karaçam & Pulur, 2017; Myers et al., 2012). The cumulative roles of unstructured and formal learnings, mentorship and officiating coaching, positive and encouraging evaluation, previous successful officiating performances and challenging officiating appointments, and advice and social community derived from other officials all provide crucial *sources* for enhancing officials' self-efficacy.

Communication/Inter-Personal Skills

Officials' communication during sport games can influence how competent and legitimate they are perceived (Cunningham, Simmons, & Mascarenhas, 2018; Mellick, Bull, Laugharne, & Fleming, 2005) and has
effects on athletes' performance (Bar-Eli, Levy-Kolker, Pie, & Tenenbaum, 1995) and motivation to transgress during competition (Faccenda, Pantaléon, & Reynes, 2009). Communicating effectively with
other sport participants (i.e., players, coaches, other officials) therefore remains a crucial set of qualities, attitudes, and skills in officials –
characteristics and competencies that differ between individuals. For
example, personal qualities in officials are often linked to effective game
management and conflict resolution, although sometimes conceived as
an elusive and stable 'X-factor' trait that only some officials possess
(a talent identification factor in officials' game appointment and career
pathway acceleration; Cunningham, Simmons, Mascarenhas, & Redhead, 2014). While sports are good at helping officials develop 'one-
way' communication skills (e.g., signaling mechanics, self-presentation,
and communicating decisions), sports find more higher-order 'two-way'
communication skills (e.g., social/situation monitoring and interaction
skills) more difficult to train (Cunningham et al., 2014). For example,
officials are said to benefit from adapting their interaction to conflict
situations by shifting between avoiding, forcing, accommodating, compromising, and collaborating styles (Mascarenhas, O'Hare, & Plessner,
2006). As a malleable functional constraint, such humanistic capacities
are perhaps more predominantly developed over life-span experiences,
constructed in early age through social relations with significant others,
and transferred from other occupational and practice context. But, similarly, these capacities are adaptable and can be refined through certain
experiences and deliberate practice (Simmons & Cunningham, 2013).

Emotional Self-Regulation

Another individual and malleable functional constraint on sport officials is self-regulation and interpersonal emotional regulation. In officiating environments synonymous for heightened emotional responses
and expectation, officials can differ in their ability to be resilient and
perform effectively under such pressures. Coping with stressors of officiating can yield different strategies by officials (i.e., problem-focused
versus emotion-focused; Voight, 2009). Indeed, anxious officials might
be more easily influenced by external factors, such as crowd noise (Sors
et al., 2019). Sometimes more classically termed, 'emotional intelligence'
(EI) – a capacity to monitor one's own and others emotions, and ultimately reason and manage such emotional responses – is said to help
officials buffer the effects of such environmental stressors. Athletes pick

up on these subtle emotional cues in officials and can perceive them as fairer and more competent when decisions are delivered in a calm tone compared to angrily (Simmons, 2010). High self-assessed EI abilities in officials are associated with better physical fitness levels (Nurcahya et al., 2019), reduced symptoms of burnout (Alam et al., 2012), and communication skill and stress levels (Nikbakhsh, Alam, & Monazami, 2013). As an individual factor in officiating performance and development, the malleable constraint of self-regulation plays a critical role in skill production, interactions with others in the sporting climate, and commitments to developmental self-learnings and progression.

Motivation

Motivation is another functional constraint that is highly malleable and that can vary between and within individuals. Officials can maintain different levels and sources of motivation (i.e., intrinsic and extrinsic) and further be motivated to officiate differently depending on their developmental period. Some enter officiating as retired players from their sport and/or want to stay involved for the love of the sport. Officiating as a leisure activity is another main motivator, while others see officiating as a way of giving back to their sport or community. Others have little choice, and independent of their motivation (extrinsic, intrinsic, or amotivation) must officiate, as in the case of high-performance squash athletes who often have to officiate their own tournaments. Commitment and identification as an official can motivate participation through a sense of community drawn from social interactions with sport participants (Hancock, Dawson, & Auger, 2015) and other officials (particularly within officiating teams). One study had officials report on their experiences of 'passion' to officiate their given sport highlighting positive experiences and emotional states and functioning during sport matches, or more optimal 'flow' experiences (Philippe, Vallerand, Andrianarisoa, & Brunel, 2009). Less passionate officials may lack these experiences influencing their performance and development (and possibly satisfaction and commitment). Extrinsic sources of motivation to officiating can include recognition, praise, advancement/promotion, and pay. Younger officials (more so than older officials) can be motivated by money when combined with a desire to also be involved in their sport (Forbes and Livingston, 2013). In other instances, extrinsic rewards such as compensation may not always be a central motivator to officiating at later developmental periods unless it is more salary-based compared to match-to-match compensation (where salary can be a better predictor of performance; Bryson et al., 2001). The point made here is that officials can have different intrinsic and extrinsic rewards and motivations to participate that actively predict one important individual constraint.

Officials can also be motivated differently based on the development period they participate. Borrowed from athlete development, the FTEM model of officiating development (MacMahon et al., 2015) suggests three main participatory motivators prior to arriving at the elite pathway: Active leisure, sport participation, and expertise advancement. Upon entry into sport, officials often are 'occasional' having casual involvement while acquiring basic rule knowledge about their sport. Officials can be motivated to develop their rule knowledge and to apply such knowledge in a new judgment task. In the following stage, officials may be motivated by active leisure where both participation opportunities and evaluation of performance increase. As such, officials are driven to more real-world application of earlier learnings and physical activity benefits that accompany this development level. Finally, as officials progress to elite pathways through advancement, they become more motivated to seek more specialized skills training and commitment increases for professionalization.

Perceptual-Cognitive Skills

Perceptual cognitive skills are an excellent example of malleable functional constraints. These skills include pattern recognition, pattern recall, anticipation, and decision-making skills. Research suggests these skills are not the result of innate capacities, but the product of extensive domain-specific training and experience. For example, Helsen and Starkes (1999) found no differences in general capacities like central and peripheral vision or reaction time between soccer athletes of different skill levels. However, there were significant differences between the groups on perceptual-cognitive tasks that were soccer specific. Through extensive experience and practice, experts are better able to recognize and process relevant information (Allard, Graham, & Paarsalu, 1980; Starkes, 1987), which is then used to inform future decisions and/or movements (Abernethy, 1986, 1990; Müller & Abernethy, 2012). Indeed, experts are better able to prioritize and allocate their gaze behavior to task-relevant information sources and hold their gaze on these locations for longer durations compared to less skilled performers (Gegenfurtner, Lehtinen, & Säljö, 2011; Kredel, Vater, Klostermann, & Hossner, 2017; Mann, Williams, Ward, & Janelle, 2007). Overall, research suggests that when experts are provided with domain-specific information, they use perceptual-cognitive skills developed over years of experience to exploit contextual information and facilitate performance.

Refined perceptual-cognitive skills are at the root of effective decision-making and officiating performance (Catteeuw, Helsen, Gilis, & Wagemans, 2009; Pietraszewski, Maszczyk, Roczniok, Golas, & Stanula, 2014). Officiating sports where there are many external cues to consider when making decisions require officials to be more attuned to perceptual cues and process them with better proficiency and attention. One perceptual constraint can be 'vision' – particularly depending on the complexity of decision cues officials are required to process (e.g., a leg before wicket decision in cricket umpiring versus adjudging the scrum in rugby union). In fact, officials' eye gaze behavior and patterns (or scanning strategies) can be different depending on experience. More elite officials can be superior in perceptual skills such as peripheral vision and speed of shape recognition that contribute to a heightened sensitivity to environment cues – but sometimes no differences can be detected between novice and more experienced officials' gaze behavior (Hancock & Ste-Marie, 2013). Individual factors other than perceptual skills act as a functional constraint on officials, including other information processing in categorization in penalty detection, memory, and prior knowledge, and how information is integrated (e.g., penalty severity). Other modelling of officials' decisions suggests that individuals can apply different underlying reasoning and explanation of cues they used to reach a decision (Mascarenhas & Smith, 2011).

A considerable body of literature has focused on the decision-making of sport officials, often with an emphases on biases or decision-making errors. Many of these studies consider the intersection between environmental factors (like crowd noise and size, home versus away teams, team nationality, or uniform colors: Constantinou, Fenton, & Pollock, 2014; Dohmen & Sauermann, 2015; Hagemann, Strauss, & Leißing, 2008; Riedl, Bernd, Heuer, & Rubner, 2015), or individual factors like positioning (e.g., Oliveira, Orbetelli, & Barros, 2011; Oudejans et al., 2000) and prior judgments (e.g., Plessner & Betsch, 2001; Schwarz, 2011). Reviewing the entire body of literature on perceptual-cognitive skill of sport officials, and biases in perceptual-cognitive skills, is beyond the scope of this chapter.

The point we wish to highlight, however, is that these skills are malleable and the result of domain-specific training and experience (Mac-Mahon, Helsen, Starkes, Cuypers, & Weston, 2007). The extent to which biases and errors in judgments exist can therefore be addressed through developmental programs, training, and increased experiential learning opportunities. In short, optimal learning environments have a direct impact on the development of these malleable skills.

Unstable Functional Constraints

While malleable constraints are adaptable by nature, unstable functional constraints are more transient, perhaps unpredictable, and emphasize the day-to-day variations that influence performance. Unlike long-term psychological factors that impact and are impacted by training (i.e., self-efficacy), daily mood can be influenced by a wide range of factors within and outside of sport. Most notably, for officials within sport these can include interactions with parents, coaches, and athletes, but equally with league administrators, match assigners, supervisors, evaluators, and other officials. Outside-of-sport influences can include interactions and events related to things like family, friends, and work-related factors. One's mood and state of emotion can impact visual perception, visual field, anticipated action, and information that can be readily and immediately used for cognitive processing (Zadra & Clore, 2012). As well, emotional arousal can enhance the learning process (Hu et al., 2007; Wolfe, 2006). Conversely, perceived mental fatigue can decrease the ability to exert cognitive control, as well as performance on cardiovascular and strength-based tasks (Bray, Martin-Ginis, Hicks, & Woodgate, 2008, Brown & Bray, 2017; Dorris, Power, & Kenefick, 2012; Englert & Wolff, 2015; Graham, Martin-Ginis, & Bray, 2017; MacMahon, Schücker, Hagemann, & Strauss, 2014; Marcora, Staiano, & Manning, 2009; Zering, Brown, Graham, & Bray, 2017). There are also indications that mental fatigue can increase distractibility (Englert, Bertrams, Furley, & Oudejans, 2015). Thus, one's current emotion, mood, and perceived psychological state may be mediators of important environmental cues in learning and match-officiating performance. Moreover, the fact that unstable functional constraints can originate from multiple sources reinforces the need for research and models of officiating science to incorporate the intersection of multiple layers (sport and non-sport) of officials' developmental ecology. Going forward, there may be a need to more clearly differentiate between officiating performance outcomes that result from malleable versus unstable functional constraints, and environmental constraints.

Implications for Performance and Development

Ultimately, we hope that classifying structural and functional characteristics as stable, malleable, and unstable provides a useful way of considering the inherent variations that can exist within sport officials. We certainly do not contend that all of the classifications we have discussed throughout this chapter apply to all officiating tasks. Far from it. For example, stable and malleable structural constraints may simply be inconsequential to effective or exceptional officiating for some sport judges (e.g., gymnastics, figure skating, or track and field). Rather, we feel that it is essential for sport organizations and practitioners to consider which individual constraints align with the sport-specific task constraints (i.e., officiating specific roles and demands; see Chapter 5).

In addition to broadly identifying which individual constraints are relevant on a sport-specific basis, it is also important to consider intra-sport variations. For example, different optimal performance profiles may differ depending on the level of sport being officiated. This may ultimately depend on how organizations and practitioners define optimal or exceptional officiating at grassroots, competitive and elite levels of play. In creating performance profiles, it may also be important to consider inter-individual variations in what constitutes an exceptional official. For a specific sport, at a specific level of attainment, *what are the different permutations and combination of skills, abilities, and characteristics that exist within an officiating population?* To our knowledge, this type of variation needs to be explored.

Once performance profiles are mapped (see Mascarenhas et al., 2005) for different sports or types of officiating task (see Chapter 5), the classifications described in this chapter can be of further use. Specifically, understanding if relevant individual constraints are stable or malleable may dictate their utility. Stable constraints (e.g., personality traits) may be more useful when identifying potentially talented officials or deciding the limits of an official's potential. Conversely, malleable constraints that are key performance factors are more likely to be target areas for development plans and training programs. Some unstable factors (e.g., mental fatigue and injury) may also be possible to incorporate into officiating development plans, while others may be useful for understanding inter- and intra-individual variations in officiating performance. When considering different types of individual constraints, these factors should be considered across time, from micro-level (immediate, on-ground daily training, and performance environments) to macro-level (long-term training programs, policies, and resource allocation) to better facilitate the development and performance of officials.

TAKE AWAY MESSAGES FROM THIS CHAPTER

- Classifying sport officials' individual characteristics into structural and functional categories helps distinguish variation in constraints on officials' performance and developmental trajectories (as they are relevant to the type of sport officiated).
- *Structural constraints* refer to those official characteristics that include bodily structures, such as anthropometric and physiological characteristics (e.g., height, weight, muscle mass).
- *Functional constraints* refer to official characteristics that are more modifiable factors in officials, such as fitness, strength, knowledge, perceptual-cognitive skill, and certain psychological characteristics.
- Each of these categories can be further categorized based on their stability, malleability, and predictability.
- Stable characteristics (structural or functional) are officials' attributes that do not predominantly vary over time (i.e., height and personality type).

(Continued)

- Malleable characteristics (structural or functional) concern aspects of officials' attributes that adapt to the demands of the task through training and experience (e.g., aerobic capacity and perceptual-cognitive skill). These characteristics are at the heart of training agendas for sport officials.
- Unstable characteristics (structural and functional) are more unpredictable factors over time that can influence performance and development progression (e.g., physical injury or mood).

Utility of a Constraints View for Sport officials' Development

- It helps account for controllability of factors (things that can be fostered in officials from outside influences, and what things are more fixed, stable, and less adaptive) in development planning, training design, and program evaluation.
- It is important to acknowledge how variations in officials' characteristics are a product of the sport-type, role, and level they function.
- Considering the spectrum of constraints and variation in official characteristics can assist in talent identification and development for advancing officials.

Notes

1 If severe enough, a prior injury could become a stable structural constraint.
2 In this context, personality traits refer to the five-factor model (or 'Big Five'): Openness, Conscientiousness, Extraversion, Agreeableness, and Neuroticism (see Pervin, Cervone, & John, 2005 for definitions).
3 Influencing the strength and/or direction of the relationship between other variables.

References

Abbott, A., Button, C., Pepping, G.J., & Collins, D. (2005). Unnatural selection: Talent identification and development in sport. *Nonlinear Dynamics, Psychology, and Life Sciences, 9,* 61–88.

Abernethy, B. (1986). Anticipation in sport: A review. *Physical Education Review, 10(1),* 5–16.

Abernethy, B. (1990). Expertise, visual search, and information pick-up in squash. *Perception, 19(1),* 63–77.

Aeron, S., & Pathak, S. (2012). Personality, cohesion and performance. *Metamorphosis, 11,* 6–26.

Alam, S., Mombeni, H., Maleki, B., Monazami, M., Alam, Z., Vatandoust, M., & Nasirzade, A. (2012). The relationship between emotional intelligence and burnout in Iranian soccer super league referees. *Current Research Journal of Biological Sciences, 4*(5), 544–550.

Alker, H.A., Straub, W.F., & Leary, J. (1973). Achieving consistency: A study of basketball officiating. *Journal of Vocational Behavior, 3*, 335–343.

Allard, F., Graham, S., & Paarsalu, M.E. (1980). Perception in sport: Basketball. *Journal of Sport Psychology, 2(1)*, 14–21.

Araújo, D., & Davids, K. (2009). Ecological approaches to cognition and action in sport and exercise: Ask not only what you do, but where you do it. *International Journal of Sport Psychology, 40*(1), 5–37.

Baker, J., Cobley, S., & Schorer, J. (Eds.). (2012). Talent identification and development in sport: International perspectives. *International Journal of Sports Science & Coaching, 7*(1), 177–180.

Baker, J., Cobley, S., Schorer, J., & Wattie, N. (Eds.). (2017). *The Routledge handbook of talent identification and development in Sport*. London: Routledge.

Baker, J., Schorer, J., & Wattie, N. (2018). Compromising talent: Issues in identifying and selecting talent in sport. *Quest, 70*, 48–63.

Baker, J., Schorer, J., & Wattie, N. (2019). A proposed conceptualization of talent in sport: The first step in a long and winding road. *Psychology of Sport & Exercise, 43*, 27–33.

Balch, M.J., & Scott, D. (2007). Contrary to popular belief, Refs are people too! Personality and perceptions of officials. *Journal of Sport Behaviour, 30*, 3–20.

Bandura, A. (1997). *Self-efficacy: The exercise of control*. New York, NY: Freeman.

Bar-Eli, M., Levy-Kolker, L., Pie, J., & Tenenbaum, G. (1995). A crisis related analysis of perceived referees' behavior in competition. *Journal of Applied Sport Psychology, 7*, 63–80.

Baron, R.M., & Kenny, D.A. (1986). The moderator-mediator variable distinction in social psychological research: Conceptual, strategic, and statistical considerations. *Journal of Personality and Social Psychology, 51*, 1173–1182.

Bergeman, C.S., Chlpuer, H.M., Plomin, R., Pedersen, N.L., McClearn, G.E., Nesselroade, J.R., Costa, P.T., Jr., & McCrae, R.R. (1993). Genetic and environmental effects on openness to experience, agreeableness, and conscientiousness: An adoption/twin study. *Journal of Personality, 61*, 159–179.

Bizzini, M., Junge, A., Bahr, R., & Dvorak, J. (2009). Injuries and musculoskeletal complaints in referees – A complete survey in the top divisions of the Swiss Football league. *Clinical Journal of Sport Medicine, 19*, 95–100.

Bizzini, M., Junge, A., Bahr, R., & Dvorak, J. (2011). Injuries of football referees: A representative survey of Swiss referees officiating at all levels of play. *Scandinavian Journal of Medicine and Science in Sport, 21*, 42–47.

Bray, S.R., Martin Ginis, K.A., Hicks, A.L., & Woodgate, J. (2008). Effects of self-regulatory strength depletion on muscular performance and EMG activation. *Psychophysiology, 45*, 337–343.

Brown, D.M.Y., & Bray, S.R. (2017). Graded increases in cognitive control exertion reveal a threshold effect on subsequent physical performance. *Sport, Exercise, and Performance Psychology, 6*, 355–369.

Bouchard, C., An, P., Rice, T., Skinner, J.S., Wilmore, J.H., & Gagnon, J. (1999). Familial aggregation of VO2max response to exercise training: Results from the HERITAGE family study. *Journal of Applied Physiology, 87,* 1003–1008.

Bouchard, C., Daw, W., Rice, T., Perusse, L., Gagnon, J., & Province, M.A. (1998). Familial resemblance for VO2max in the sedentary state: The HERITAGE family study. *Medicine & Science in Sports and Exercise, 30,* 252–258.

Calvo, M., Rodas, G., Vallejo, M., Estruch, A., Arcas, A., Javierre, C., Viscor, G., & Ventura, J. (2002). Heritability of explosive power and anaerobic capacity in humans. *European Journal of Applied Physiology, 86,* 218–225.

Castagna, C., Abt, G., & D'Ottavio, S. (2007). Physiological aspects of soccer refereeing performance and training. *Sports Medicine, 37,* 625–646.

Catteeuw, P., Helsen, W., Gilis, B., & Wagemans, J. (2009). Decision-making skills, role specificity, and deliberate practice in association football refereeing. *Journal of Sports Sciences, 27*(11), 1125–1136.

Constantinou, A.C., Fenton, N.E., & Pollock, L.J.H. (2014). Bayesian networks for unbiased assessment of referee bias in Association Football. *Psychology of Sport and Exercise, 15(5),* 538–547.

Cunningham, I., Simmons, P., & Mascarenhas, D.R.D. (2018). Sport officials' strategies for managing interactions with players: Face-work on the frontstage. *Psychology of Sport and Exercise, 39,* 154–162.

Cunningham, I., Simmons, P., Mascarenhas, D., & Redhead, S. (2014). Skilled interaction: Concepts of communication and player management in the development of sport officials. *International Journal of Sport Communication, 7,* 166–187.

Dehghansai, N., Lemez, S., Wattie, N., Baker, J., & Pinder, R. (under review). Understanding the development of elite parasport athletes: Current understanding and future directions. *Frontiers in Psychology - Performance Science.*

Dohmen, T., & Sauermann, J. (2015). Referee bias. *Journal of Economic Surveys,* 1–17. doi:10.1111/joes.12106.

Dorris, D.C., Power, D.A., & Kenefick, E. (2012). Investigating the effects of ego depletion on physical exercise routines of athletes. *Psychology of Sport and Exercise, 13,* 118–125.

Dosseville, F., Laborde, S., & Bernier, M. (2014). Athletes' expectations with regards to officiating competence. *European Journal of Sport Science, 14,* S448–S455.

Englert, C., Bertrams, A., Furley, P., & Oudejans, R.R.D. (2015). Is ego depletion associated with increased distractibility? Results from a basketball free throw task. *Psychology of Sport and Exercise, 18,* 26–31.

Englert, C., & Wolff, W. (2015). Ego depletion and persistent performance in a cycling task. *International Journal of Sport Psychology, 6,* 137–151.

Faccenda, L., Pantaléon, N., & Reynes, E. (2009). Significant predictors of soccer players' moral functioning from components of contextual injustice, sensitivity to injustice and moral atmosphere. *Social Justice Research, 22,* 399–415.

Feltz, D.L, Short, S.E., & Sullivan, P.J. (2008). *Self-efficacy in sport: Research and strategies for working with athletes, teams, and coaches.* Champaign, IL: Human Kinetics.

Forbes, A., Edwards, L., & Fleming, S. (2015). 'Women can't referee': exploring the experiences of female football officials within UK football culture. *Soccer & Society, 16*(4), 521–539.

Forbes, S.L., & Livingston, L.A. (2013). Changing the call: Rethinking attrition and retention in the ice hockey officiating ranks. *Sport in Society, 16*(3), 295–309.

Fratzke, M.R. (1975). Personality and biographical traits of superior and average college basketball officials. *The Research Quarterly, 46*, 484–488.

Gabrilo, G., Ostojic, M., Idrizovic, K., Novosel, B., & Sekulic, D. (2013). A retrospective survey on injuries in Croatian football/soccer referees. *BMC Musculoskeletal Disorders, 14*, 88.

Gegenfurtner, A., Lehtinen, E., & Säljö, R. (2011). Expertise differences in the comprehension of visualizations: A meta-analysis of eye-tracking research in professional domains. *Educational Psychology Review, 23(4)*, 523–552.

Glazier, P.S., & Robins, M.T. (2013). Self-organization and constraints in sports performance. In T.G. McGarry, P. O'Donoghue, & J. Sampaio (Eds.), *The Routledge handbook of sports performance analysis* (pp. 42–51). London: Routledge.

Graham, J.D., Martin Ginis, K.A., & Bray, S.R. (2017). Exertion of self-control increases fatigue, reduces task self-efficacy, and impairs performance of resistance exercise. *Sport, Exercise, and Performance Psychology, 6*, 70–88.

Guillén, F., & Feltz, D.L. (2011). A conceptual model of referee efficacy. *Frontiers in Psychology, 2*, 25. doi:10.3389/fpsyg.2011.00025

Hagemann, N., Strauss, B., & Leißing, J. (2008). When the Referee Sees Red …. *Psychological Science, 19*, 769–771.

Hancock, D.J., Dawson, D.J., & Auger, D. (2015). Why ref? Understanding sport officials' motivations to begin, continue, and quit. *Movement & Sport Sciences-Science & Motricité, 87*, 31–39.

Hancock, D.J., Martin, L.J., Evans, M.B., & Paradis, K.F. (2018). Exploring perceptions of group processes in ice hockey officiating. *Journal of Applied Sport Psychology, 30*(2), 222–240.

Hancock, D.J., & Ste-Marie, D.M. (2013). Gaze behaviors and decision making accuracy of higher-and lower-level ice hockey referees. *Psychology of Sport and Exercise, 14*(1), 66–71.

Hardy, L., Barlow, M., Evans, L., Rees, T., Woodman, T., & Warr, C. (2017). Great British medalists: Psychosocial biographies of super-elite and elite athletes from Olympic sports. *Progress in Brain Research, 232*, 1–119.

Helsen, W., & Starkes, J.L. (1999). A multidimensional approach to skilled perception and performance in sport. *Applied Cognitive Psychology, 13*, 1–27.

Hu, H., Reak, E., Takamiya, K., Kang, M., Ledoux, J., Huganir, R.L., & Malinow, R. (2007). Emotion enhances learning via norepinephrine regulation of AMPA-Receptor trafficking. *Cell Press, 131*(1), 160–173.

Ittenbach, R.F., & Eller, B.F. (1989). The official personality. *Journal of Sport and Exercise Psychology, 11*(2), 119.

Kredel, R., Vater, C., Klostermann, A., & Hossner, E.-J. (2017). Eye-tracking technology and the dynamics of natural gaze behavior in sports: A systematic review of 40 years of research. *Frontiers in Psychology, 8*, 1845. doi:10.3389/fpsyg.2017.01845

Koz, D., Fraser-Thomas, J., & Baker, J. (2012). Accuracy of professional sports drafts in predicting career potential. *Scandinavian Journal of Medicine & Science in Sports, 22*, e64–e69.

Lirgg, C.D., Feltz, D.L., & Merrie, M.D. (2016). Self-efficacy of sports officials: A critical review of the literature. *Journal of Sport Behavior, 39*, 39–50.

Livingston, L.A., & Forbes, S L. (2016). Factors contributing to the retention of Canadian amateur sport officials: Motivations, perceived organizational support, and resilience. *International Journal of Sports Science & Coaching, 11*(3), 342–355.

Livingston, L.A., Forbes, S.L., Wattie, N., Pearson, N., Camacho, T., & Varian, P. (2017). Sport officiating recruitment, development, and retention: A call to action. *Current Issues in Sport Science, 2*(11). doi: 10.15203/CISS_2017.011

MacMahon, C., Helsen, W.F., Starkes, J.L., Cuypers, K., & Weston, M. (2007). Decision-making skills and deliberate practice in elite association football referees. *Journal of Sport Sciences, 25*, 65–78.

MacMahon, C., Schücker, L., Hagemann, N., & Strauss, B. (2014). Cognitive fatigue effects on physical performance during running. *Journal of Sport & Exercise Psychology, 36*, 375–381.

MacMahon, C., Mascarenhas, D., Plessner, H., Pizzera, A., Oudejans, R., & Raab, M. (2015). Development of sports officials (pp. 8–32). In *Sports officials and officiating: Science and Practice*. London: Routledge.

Maddux, J. (Ed.). (1995). Self-efficacy theory: An introduction. In *Self-efficacy, adaptation, and adjustment: Theory, research, and application* (pp. 3–33). New York: Plenum Press.

Mann, D.T.Y., Williams, A.M., Ward, P., & Janelle, C.M. (2007). Perceptual-cognitive expertise in sport: A meta-analysis. *Journal of Sport and Exercise Psychology, 29(4)*, 457–478.

Marcora, S.M., Staiano, W., & Manning, V. (2009). Mental fatigue impairs physical performance in humans. *Journal of Applied Physiology, 106*, 857–864.

Mascarenhas, D.R.D., Collins, D., & Mortimer, P. (2005). Elite refereeing performance: Developing a model for sport science support. *The Sport Psychologist, 19*, 364–379.

Mascarenhas, D.R.D., O Hare, D., & Plessner, H. (2006). The psychological and performance demands of association football refereeing. *International Journal of Sport Psychology, 37*(2/3), 99–120.

Mascarenhas, D.R.D. & Smith, N.C. (2011). Developing the performance brain: Decision making under pressure. In D. Collins, H. Richards & C. Button (Eds.), *Performance psychology – Developing a peak performance culture* (pp. 245–267). Edinburgh: Elsevier.

McEvoy, B.P., & Visscher, P.M. (2009). Genetics of human height. *Economics & Human Biology, 7*, 294–306.

Mellick, M., Bull, P., Laugharne, E., & Fleming, S. (2005). Identifying best practice for referee decision communication in association and rugby union football: A microanalytic approach. *Football Studies, 8*, 42–57.

Müller, S., & Abernethy, B. (2012). Expert anticipatory skill in striking sports: A review and a model. *Research Quarterly for Exercise and Sport, 83(2)*, 175–187.

Myers, N.D., Feltz, D.L., Guillén, F., & Dithurbide, L. (2012). Development of, and initial validity evidence for, the reference self-efficacy scale: A multistudy report. *Journal of Sport & Exercise Psychology, 34*, 737–765.

Newell, K.M. (1986). Constraints on the development of coordination. In M.G. Wade & H.T.A. Whiting (Eds.), *Motor development in children: Aspects of coordination and control* (pp. 341–361). Amsterdam: Martin Nijhoff.

Newell, K.M., Liu, Y.T., & Mayer-Kress, G. (2001). Time scales in motor learning and development. *Psychological Review*, 108, 57–82.

Newell, K.M., Mayer-Kress, G., Hong, S.L., & Liu, Y.T. (2009). Adaptation and learning: Characteristic time scales of performance dynamics. *Human Movement Science*, 28, 655–687.

Newell, K.M., Mayer-Kress, G., Hong, S.L., & Liu, Y.T. (2010). Decomposing the performance dynamics of learning through time scales. In P.C.M. Molenaar & K.M. Newell (Eds.), *Individual Pathways of Changes in Learning & Development* (pp. 71–86). Washington, DC: American Psychological Association.

Nikbakhsh, R., Alam, S., & Monazami, M. (2013). The relationship between emotional intelligence, communication skills and stress among Iranian premier league referees. *Annals of Biological Research*, 4(4), 196–203.

Norton, K., & Olds, T. (2001). Morphological evolution of athletes over the 20th century: Causes and consequences. *Sports Medicine*, 31, 763–783.

Nurcahya, Y., Mulyana, D., & Sagitarius, S. (2019, September). Relationship between emotional intelligence and physical fitness with football referee performance. In *3rd International Conference on Sport Science, Health, and Physical Education (ICSSHPE 2018)*. Atlantis Press.

Oliveira, M., Reis, L., & Inácio, A. (2016). Injury incidence in Brazilian football referees. *Archivos de Medicina Del Deporte*, 33(2), 108–112.

Oudejans, R.R.D., Verheijen, R., Bakker, R.F., Gerrits, J.C., Steinbrückner, M., & Beek, P.J. (2000). Errors in judging 'offside' in football. *Nature*, 404, 33.

Penke, L., Denissen, J. J., & Miller, G. F. (2007). The evolutionary genetics of personality. *European Journal of Personality: Published for the European Association of Personality Psychology*, 21(5), 549–587.

Pervin, L.A., Cervone, D., & John, O.P. (2005). *Personality: Theory and research* (9th ed.). Hoboken, NJ: John Wiley.

Philippe, F.L., Vallerand, R.J., Andrianarisoa, J., & Brunel, P. (2009). Passion in referees: Examining their affective and cognitive experiences in sport situations. *Journal of Sport and Exercise Psychology*, 31(1), 77–96.

Pietraszewski, P., Maszczyk, A., Roczniok, R., Golas, A., & Stanula, A. (2014). Differentiation of perceptual processes in elite and assistant soccer referees. *Procedia - Social and Behavioral Sciences*, 117, 469–474. doi:10.1016/j.sbspro.2014.

Pina, J.A., Passos, A., Araújo, D., & Maynard, M.T. (2018). Football refereeing: An integrative review. *Psychology of Sport & Exercise*, 35, 10–26.

Pizzera, A. (2015). The role of embodied cognition in sports officiating. *Movement & Sport Sciences-Science & Motricité*, 87, 53–61.

Plessner, H., & Betsch, T. (2001). Sequential effects in important referee decisions: The case of penalties in soccer. *Journal of Sport and Exercise Psychology*, 23, 254–259.

Rankinen, T,, Bray, M.S., Hagberg, J.M., Pérusse, L., Roth, S.M., Wolfarth, B., & Bouchard, C. (2006). The human gene map for performance and health-related fitness phenotypes: The 2005 update. *Medicine & Science in Sports & Exercise*, 38, 1863–1888.

Riedl, D., Bernd, S., Heuer, A., & Rubner, O. (2015). Finale furioso: Referee-biased injury times and their effects on home advantage in football. *Journal of Sports Sciences*, 33(4), 327–336. doi:10.1080/02640414.2014.944558

Robinson, K., Wattie, N., Schorer, J., & Baker, J. (2018). Talent identification in sport: A systematic review of 25 years of research. *Sports Medicine, 48,* 97–109.

Sayfollahpour, P., Ganjooee, F. A., & Nikbakhsh, R. (2013). The relationship between personality and performance of football referees. *International Journal of Academic Research in Business and Social Sciences, 3*(9), 1–6.

Schwarz, W. (2011). Compensating tendencies in penalty kick decisions of referees in professional football: Evidence from the German Bundesliga 1963–2006. *Journal of Sports Sciences, 29*(5), 441–447.

Sharpe, S., Synnott, A., Cunningham, I., & Ordway, C. (2019, July). Demand for early recruitment and faster development. Presentation at the *European Federation of Sport and Exercise Psychology Congress.* University of Münster, Germany.

Simmons, P. (2010). Communicative displays as fairness heuristics: Strategic football referee communication. *Australian Journal of Communication, 37,* 75–94.

Simmons, P. (2011). Competent, dependable and respectful: Football 402 refereeing as a model for communicating fairness. *Ethical Space: The International Journal of Communication Ethics, 8,* 33–42.

Simmons, P., & Cunningham, I. (2013). Communication and sport officials. In P.M. Pedersen (Ed.), *Routledge handbook of sport communication* (pp. 461–470). London: Routledge.

Smith, M.M., Sherry, S.B., Vidovic, V., Saklofske, D.H., Stoeber, J., & Benoit, A. (2019). Perfectionism and the five-factor model of personality: A meta-analytic review. *Personality and Social Psychology Review, 23,* 367–390.

Sors, F., Tomé Lourido, D., Parisi, V., Santoro, I., Galmonte, A., Agostini, T.A., & Murgia, M. (2019). Pressing crowd noise impairs the ability of anxious basketball referees to discriminate fouls. *Frontiers in Psychology, 10,* 2380.

Starkes, J.L. (1987). Skill in field hockey: The nature of the cognitive advantage. *Journal of Sport Psychology, 9(2),* 146–160.

Tingle, J. K., Warner, S., & Sartore-Baldwin, M.L. (2014). The experience of former women officials and the impact on the sporting community. *Sex Roles, 71*(1–2), 7–20.

Voight, M. (2009). Sources of stress and coping strategies of US soccer officials. *Stress and Health: Journal of the International Society for the Investigation of Stress, 25*(1), 91–101.

Wattie, N., & Baker, N. (2018). An uneven playing field: Talent identification systems and the perpetuation of participation biases in high performance sport. In R. Dionigi & M. Gard (Eds.), *Sport and physical activity across the lifespan: Critical perspectives.* Macmillan.

Wolfe, P. (2006). The role of meaning and emotion in learning. *New Directions for Adult & Continuing Education, 110,* 35–41.

Zadra, J.R., & Clore, G.L. (2011). Emotion and perception: The role of affective information. *Wiley Interdisciplinary Reviews: Cognitive Science, 2*(6), 676–685.

Zering, J.C., Brown, D.M., Graham, J.D., & Bray, S.R. (2017). Cognitive control exertion leads to reductions in peak power output and as well as increased perceived exertion on a graded exercise test to exhaustion. *Journal of Sports Sciences, 35,* 1799–1807.

5 All Sports Are Not Created Equal

Identifying the Complexities of the Officiating Task

A quick search of the World Wide Web, including commercial book selling websites, yields a long list of print resources related to sport officiating. Some are generic in nature, focusing on information and required skillsets common to all officiating roles (e.g., ethics and professionalism, game or competition assignments, communication skills) (e.g., Clegg & Thompson, 1985; Davis, 1996) or population-based officiating considerations such as youth sport or women's sport (e.g., Mackey & Mackey, 1964; Still, 2000). In contrast, many others – perhaps the majority – concentrate on sport-specific skillsets and responsibilities (e.g., rulebooks and rule interpretations, physical and psychological demands of the sport, positioning or scoring systems) (e.g., Korth, 2015; McEvoy, 2002; Stern, 2002). This is understandable given that every sport official must have a full understanding of the rules and the technical aspects of their application for their given sport. There are also several autobiographical works available, largely from retired professional officials in mainstream sports such as ice hockey, football, and baseball, which focus on the highs and the lows, as well as the hilarious and the not-so-flattering moments of their careers (e.g., Hood, 1989; Pallone & Steinberg, 1990; Pereira & Jaffe, 2016; Postema & Wojciechowski, 1992). More recently, a large number of self-published e-books offering anecdotal tips on how to deal with the challenges of being an official have emerged.

Very few published texts, in contrast, explicitly attempt to bridge the gap between what we know about officiating from an evidence-informed scientific point of view to the practice of it as a profession. In some ways, this is not surprising given that officials have until recently received little attention from the sport science community. The volume of scientific work from which evidence-based insights may be drawn is consequently limited. This is a problem of quantity. However, there is also a challenge related to the quality of efforts undertaken to date. As Hancock and his co-authors (2015) explain, the lack of adherence to theoretical frameworks has led to a disconnected collection of officiating studies that are sport- and population-specific, methodologically diverse, narrowly focused, and short on detail. Stated another way, up until now, we have tended to study officiating by removing it from the real-world context in which it happens. The use of theoretical frameworks and adherence to sound research methodologies are essential if we want to effectively and systematically link theory to practice going forward. Throughout this text, we emphasize the need to utilize an approach (or theoretical framework) that recognizes the multiple factors (i.e., as they relate to the individual, the task, and the environment) contributing to each distinct sport officiating role. Just as individual officials differ from one another (see Chapter 4), so too do the sports they oversee, as well as the environments (see Chapter 6) in which they are required to perform. Overt recognition that the nature of sport officiating tasks varies considerably between and within sports is essential if the demands placed on any individual in a given role are to be understood and accurately assessed.

Consider, for example, how vastly different the task of being an umpire in women's field lacrosse is from that of being a judge in figure skating. The lacrosse umpire moves within a 110 m long by 60 m wide field of play amongst 24 competitors, divided equally between two teams and moving in opposite directions. The action is fast-paced, with each team focused on gaining possession of and eventually depositing a ball into their opponent's goal cage. The umpire must be physically fit and able to move with and change direction at the same pace as the athletes while constantly repositioning to see the play, communicating with their officiating partners, and blowing a whistle to make the appropriate calls. The figure skating judge, in contrast, sits next to the ice surface outside the structural confines of the ice rink, separated from the athletes and the surrounding crowd. He or she, along with fellow judges, occupies a stationary unobstructed viewing position while monitoring the skaters' performance against detailed complex standards, with only one skater or skating team occupying the ice surface at any given time. These officiating tasks are both demanding yet starkly different, and are but one of an endless number of officiating task comparisons that we could have chosen to illustrate this assertion. The key points are that the demands placed on an official are inherently and inextricably associated with the nature and requirements of the sport in which they are participating, as well as the specific role they are fulfilling during any match or competition (e.g., match official/referee versus linesmen/assistants; timer versus scorekeeper). Understanding these demands is important if optimal methods of training officials to occupy specific roles are to be developed.

Creating a classification scheme to understand the common elements experienced by all officials, as well as to capture both the complexity and the diversity of officiating tasks, is not an easy exercise. To do so we began with Plessner and MacMahon's (2013) two dimensional model, which, to the best of our knowledge, is the only one appearing in the sport officiating literature to date that overtly attempts to categorize sport officials based on the demands of the role they occupy. It provides a useful foundation for discussions, but as these authors acknowledge themselves, there is still a great deal to understand about the demands placed on sport officials. They also speak openly about their model being a starting point and that additional requirements of the role are not explicitly captured in their classification scheme. As a second step, we examined existing taxonomic classification schemes used in the scientific study of sport. Taxonomic classification refers to the process of naming and classifying things or concepts into groups according to their similarities and differences. These systems are commonly used in the biological sciences to provide a logical approach to the study of plants and animals, yet their use in sport contexts is probably more common than one might think. Importantly, we identified two existing sport classification schemes to further guide our thinking. The first emerges from the well-known Teaching Games for Understanding (TGfU) approach to physical education curricula and athlete development that emphasizes the importance of learning the logic of play imposed by the rules as well as an appreciation of tactical play structures of like games before placing emphasis on the acquisition of highly technical sport-specific skills. The second, Stefani's (1999) taxonomy of sport rating systems, groups all sports into three overarching categories based on the fundamental nature of each sport and the question of what different sports have in common. In the following sections, we individually summarize the key elements of these three classification schemes, consider other factors not explicitly addressed in the same, and follow with a newly proposed model in an effort to explain the common elements while at the same time capturing the complexity, diversity, and range of officiating tasks.

Plessner and MacMahon's (2013) Classification of Officials

In developing their model of sport officials, Plessner and MacMahon (2013) begin by acknowledging that officials are an essential yet complex group of sport participants whose performance requires acknowledging the variety of demands placed on them. They suggest that four key dimensions (i.e., knowledge and rule application, contextual judgment, personality and game management, and physical fitness) explain the majority of variation between differing officiating roles. They also propose three general categories of officials based on the intersection of two key competition elements, that is the number of athletes or external cues (e.g., perceptual, informational) requiring monitoring and the movement demands and amount of interaction they have with athletes during competition (Figure 5.1). These include:

- Interactors: Often a large number of cues to process with high interaction and physical movement demands (e.g., field lacrosse umpire).
- Monitors: Often a medium to large number of cues to monitor with lower to medium interaction and physical demands (e.g., figure skating judge).

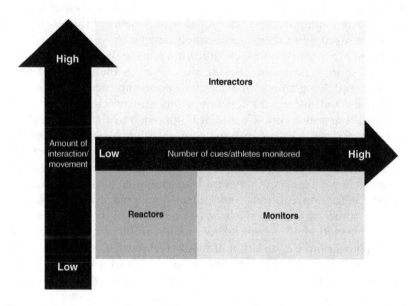

Figure 5.1 Plessner and MacMahon's (2013) classification of sport officials based on movement, interaction, and perceptual demands.

• Reactors: A low to medium number of cues to track with low inter-action and movement demands (e.g., tennis line judge). (MacMahon et al., 2014, p. 9).

Importantly, this simple conceptualization places an explicit emphasis on quantifying the interaction between the physical (i.e., movement, positioning, proximity to athletes, and mechanics) and cognitive (i.e., perceptual processing, decision-making) demands of the officiating task. More implicitly, however, the terms "reactor" and "monitor" also imply that there is a temporal element embodied within the decision-making process, while the term 'interactor' can imply a heightened communication component.

Teaching Games for Understanding Taxonomies

The Teaching Games for Understanding (TGfU) approach evolved out a movement in the 1960s away from teaching sport skills by means of a drill approach to the use of sport-related games (e.g., small-sided games). At the heart of the TGfU method was the concept of game categories, or the grouping of games based on the logic of play imposed by the rules as well as an appreciation of like tactical play structures (see Figure 5.2). In the early stages, games were simply grouped into three categories (i.e., net, batting, or running) based on whether the objective was to send an object

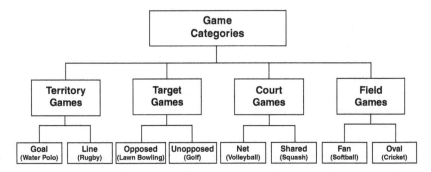

Figure 5.2 Ellis' (1983) four category and eight subcategory game classification scheme (with examples).

away, gain possession of an object, or travel with an object (Mauldon & Redfern, 1969). Ellis (1983) later expanded and refined game classification to include four categories (i.e., territory, target, court, and field) and eight subcategories (defined by game characteristics such as scoring into a goal or by crossing a line, actions opposed or not opposed by a competitor, sharing the playing area with an opponent or not, and the shape of the play area).

The grouping of games based on common logic, objectives, tactics, and structures (e.g., playing areas in terms of shape, size, and whether shared or unshared with competitors) adds a dimension of complexity to the officiating experience. It also builds on the movement and interaction, and perceptual dimensions, of Plessner and MacMahon's (2013) classification model by adding contextual elements to the discussion. These contextual elements are important in creating an ecologically valid conceptualization of the sport official's role. They may also help to explain why previous experience as an athlete may assist in the development of officiating expertise in the same or a similar sport, and support the value of training and mentoring officials in naturalistic settings (e.g., practice scrimmages, games, and competitions) in addition to classrooms and fitness tests.

Stefani's (1999) Taxonomy of Sport Rating Systems

In our previous research on sport officials (e.g., Livingston & Forbes, 2016), we used Stefani's taxonomy of sport rating systems as a framework to systematically classify a comprehensive list of sports into three overarching groups (i.e., combat, object, or independent) based on the fundamental nature of each sport and the question of what different sports have in common. To define these three categories, Stefani made a critical distinction as to what each competitor was trying to control (i.e., an opponent, themselves, or an object). In our estimation, one-on-one combat sports (e.g., fencing, karate, and wrestling) coherently merge into a singular classification grouping, while independent and object sports require further subcategorization (Figure 5.3a).

Independent sports, or those characterized by minimal to no oppositional interaction with competitors (i.e., no competitor may interfere with another competitor), cluster into three subcategories as follows: Aim/projectiles, aesthetic, and racing/lifting (Figure 5.3b). With the exception of weather as a modifying factor, the environments in which these sports are conducted are relatively closed (i.e., highly stable and unchanging with defined structural dimensions, fixtures, boundaries, and distances). Competitors may compete side-by-side in a shared environment, or perform at different times or even in different locations, as individuals or as a team.

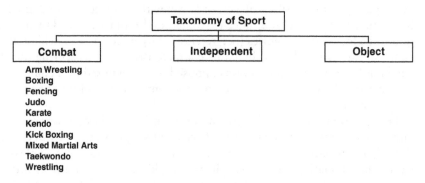

Figure 5.3a Stefani's (1999) three category taxonomy of sport: Combat sports.

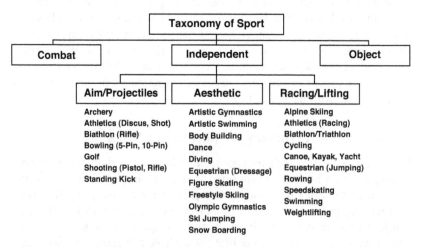

Figure 5.3b Stefani's (1999) three category taxonomy of sport: Independent and individual sports.

Object sports are those in which each competitor (or team), in the face of opposition, attempts to control an object. As is the case with independent sports, weather may be a modifying factor. However, object sport environments are more open; that is, they are dynamic in nature given constant change in object and player positions and movement. Defined by set structural dimensions, fixtures, and boundaries, they subdivide into four groupings as follows: Net/court, invasion, fielding, or target games. For each subcategory, the nature of the opposition falls somewhere on a continuum between alternating (e.g., curling where teams take turns in an effort to vie for position), intermittent (e.g., cricket where the play begins with a bowl or tennis where play begins with a serve), or constant (e.g., in invasion games like soccer and hockey) until play is stopped. The degree of interaction between competitors also varies, depending upon the nature of the competition environment. Net and court games, for example, have competitors either moving about a common competition space (e.g., squash) or divided by a net (e.g., badminton). Invasion games, by their name, imply a shared playing area in which competitors move in opposite directions to invade their opponents' territory, and score by crossing a line or depositing an object into a defined goal. Fielding games, like baseball and softball, have competitors share the space but while occupying opposing offensive or defensive roles. Target games, in contrast, require competitors to take turns in propelling objects in an effort to gain a positional or scoring advantage within a defined competition space (Figure 5.3c).

Importantly, Stefani also identifies three distinct ways in which officials evaluate performance in sport. These include the acts of judging (e.g., diving and gymnastics), measurement (i.e., by time, length, or weight as in swimming, discus, or weightlifting, respectively), and scoring

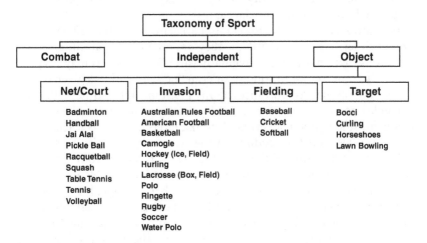

Figure 5.3c Stefani's (1999) three category taxonomy of sport: Object, target sports.

(i.e., as in baseball, tennis, and golf). He notes that these three evaluative modes are mutually exclusive, yet we suggest that more than one form of evaluation might be required of an official or team of officials in a given sport. For example, in American football, it could be argued that officials incorporate judgment in the form of interpretation (i.e., was a foul committed?), measurement (i.e., was a first down achieved?), and score (i.e., did the football cross the goal line plane?). Similarly, officials overseeing a weightlifting competition must make note of the absolute weight lifted, while also judging whether the athlete utilized proper form and held the bar in a raised, stable, and fixed position for it to be deemed a "clean" lift. Importantly, when multiple officials are involved in simultaneously monitoring various aspects of a competition, they must have clearly established processes and effective means via which they communicate with one another. Understanding the nature and extent of the evaluative and communication processes required is important if one truly wishes to understand the cognitive demands borne by officials.

Other Considerations

In our efforts to understand the demands of the officiating task, we and other sport scientists predominantly do so through a quantitative lens. Common sense, moreover, makes it easy to understand that an official who must run and keep pace with athletes on a large playing surface must be fit in order to do their job well. Similarly, it is only natural that the total number of perceptual cues arising at any given instant on a field hockey pitch populated by 22 players is greater than the same number of cues for a singular swimmer leaving the blocks at the sound of the horn to begin a race. Although not an exact science, anyone can reasonably estimate the relative quantity or overall magnitude of the physical and cognitive burdens of the officiating task.

In contrast, the affective (or emotional) demands of the officiating task are much less easy to quantify, if they are quantifiable at all, given that they are situationally and individually variable. Emotions may vary considerably from contest to contest, or even fluctuate within a given contest, depending on the circumstances at any given instant in time. Officiating a regular season game, for example, versus a singular sudden-victory championship match may evoke differing levels of stress. Officials' emotions may also vary depending on the size and proximity to spectator gallery and the nature of the verbal feedback received from the players, coaches, and others. Being able to cope with negative feedback, moreover, will differ between individuals on the bases of age, life experience, officiating experience, and perceived levels of expertise, self-confidence, and self-efficacy in the officiating role. On any given day, moreover, fatigue, injury, or a minor illness may lessen an official's ability to regulate their emotional responses. Given the variability in individual capacity to respond as well as the situational circumstances that give rise to affective task demands, they are perhaps best captured in discussions of the individual (Chapter 4) and officiating environment (Chapter 6).

A Dual Continuum Classification Scheme of Officiating Role Demands

It makes sense that newly recruited soon-to-be sport officials usually begin their training via classroom-based information sessions focused on learning the rules of their sport and how to apply them. The challenge that arises thereafter is putting that knowledge into action when first stepping into the competition environment. Being prepared to face the demands – movement (or fitness) and perceptual-cognitive – is essential for success and something that is achieved through subsequent practice, training, and experience. However, the number of practice hours officials are able to engage in is proportionally less than that of athletes. This raises questions about the other types of experiences and training that can be used to supplement officials' in-game learnings and help with this transition of knowledge to practice. Therefore, the goal is to design practice and training programs that meet the specific demands of the officiating role such that individuals may perform with success and find satisfaction in their efforts.

In conceptualizing a new classification scheme for sport officiating tasks (Figure 5.4), we have borrowed from and modified Plessner and MacMahon's (2013) classification of sport officials based on movement, interaction, and perceptual demands. In so doing, we have re-defined the two dimensions of their scheme (i.e., amount of movement and interaction with athletes; number of cues or athletes monitored) as continuums, one reflecting the officials' movement as ranging from static to dynamic while occupying a position either outside or inside the playing area. This acknowledges both the extent of movement (i.e., no movement or the static positioning of a seated artistic swimming judge compared to the constant, dynamically changing position of a soccer referee) and the relative positioning of the official outside, close to or moving in and out of, the competition area (e.g., lawn bowls umpire). Similarly, the second continuum accounts for the number of cues being monitored (i.e., number of athletes, projectiles, fellow officials), but also describes the environment and nature of play as closed (or virtually unchanging) versus open (or constantly changing). In instances where athletes are constantly on the move and an official's view of the action may be obstructed, they must rely on their technical training to either constantly re-position themselves (e.g., soccer referee) or communicate with another official (e.g., tennis line umpire) to make the call. These conceptual changes, while somewhat subtle in nature, borrow elements from the taxonomic classification of sports and are intentional in an effort to begin introducing sport-specific contextual elements into the discussion.

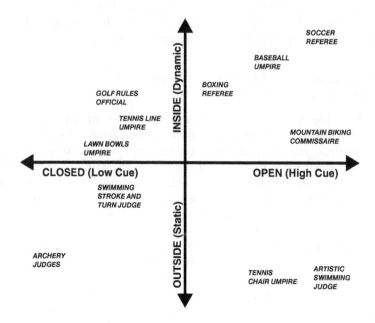

Figure 5.4 Relative classification of officiating tasks by location, movement requirements, and perceptual demands.

Our classification scheme for sport officiating tasks also differs from that of Plessner and MacMahon (2013) in that we have opted not to categorize officials as reactors, monitors, or interactors. These labels, while convenient and descriptive of the nature of the primary perceptual task carried out by a given official, may not accurately capture the full scope of an official's evaluation responsibilities or the extent of the cognitive processing or decision-making task required to convert the perceptual information gained into an actual call. Indeed, a women's field lacrosse official, in addition to interacting with 24 athletes and fellow officials within the field of play, must both quickly react to situations (e.g., by immediately blowing her whistle in response to a flagrant foul) and constantly monitor player positions (e.g., to call obstruction of free space violations). These examples from the sport of women's field lacrosse, moreover, provide a rather salient example of how constant interaction with the athletes, reaction to, and monitoring of player movement collectively contribute to the umpires' efforts to reduce the risk of injury within the game.

Equating Task Demands to Training Approaches

In any given sport, the extent to which an official must interact, monitor, or react (or evaluate as Stefani (1999) has proposed through judging, measuring, or scoring a performance) as an individual official or as a member of an officiating team is best determined by the sport's technical experts. To this end, we challenge you to insert each of the defined officiating roles for your sport within the dual continuum model. This will serve as a starting point for understanding the movement versus cognitive-perceptual demands associated with each role. From there, consider how difficult it would be for someone with no experience or knowledge of a particular sport to at that instant step into the role. Bridging the gap, with training, between how that neophyte, not yet trained official feels at that point in time versus their first formal competition can go a long way to determining their enjoyment and therefore willingness to stay in the role. Equating the demands of the role to the most appropriate training methods and approaches is essential. As a starting point in designing training programs, consider the following for officiating roles that fall within the following quadrants of the dual continuum model:

- OPEN/DYNAMIC: Roles associated with high fitness demands combined with high perceptual-cognitive decision-making responsibilities. Fitness training is essential, as is training within naturalistic environments. Importantly, this fitness training should attempt to mirror the constant changes in physical workload intensity and movement direction characteristic of the sport in question. In addition to classroom training, online modules, the use of simulated game situations, and exposure to the open/dynamic nature of the sport should begin with shadowing or immersion in practice/training games/competitions as soon as possible. Advanced perceptual-cognitive training should include opportunities to engage in decision-making while fatigued. For example, following fatiguing bouts of exercise, ask officials to respond to competition situations captured on video. Include opportunities for officials to make decisions in "above real-time" training approaches, whereby the videos are played two times faster than real-time situations to inoculate them to the attentional demands required in open/dynamic sporting environments. Scenario building exercises, as well as structured group discussions on decisions and decision reasoning, with experienced officials may also be used to prepare them for their roles.
- CLOSED/DYNAMIC: Roles associated with low to moderate fitness demands combined with moderate perceptual-cognitive decision-making requirements. Officials must be mobile and fitness training would be advantageous, particularly training that improves fitness in isolated movements or helps to relieve postural demands unique to their officiated sport. Begin with an emphasis on classroom training, online modules, and simulated competition situations, followed by gradual immersion/shadowing in competition environments.
- OPEN/STATIC: Roles associated with low fitness demands with high perceptual-cognitive decision-making requirements. Initial training

should consist of classroom training, online modules, and extensive use of video portrayals of actual performances in slow motion followed by real time. Thereafter, competition training should consist of pairing new officials with experienced officials to provide mentoring and the opportunity to shadow during competitions. Perceptual-cognitive training should emphasize the use of video-based tools for both cue learning and review to develop these type of officials' cue detection skills. While fitness training may be a lower priority, physical and postural stress related to long periods of sitting or repetitious body movements should be accounted for in recovery and training.

- CLOSED/STATIC: Roles associated with low fitness demands and because they are task-focused, the perceptual-cognitive and decision-making requirements are low. Begin with an emphasis on classroom training, online modules, and simulated competition situations, followed by gradual immersion/shadowing in competition environments.

The ultimate goal of any training program is to prepare officials to be optimally effective in performing within sport competitions. Just as athletes and coaches must learn through practice and experience, so too must officials in ways that accommodate a shortage of representative practice hours and general reliance on 'in-game' learning. Because the officiating practice environment is so unique in comparison to other sport participants, implicit and explicit types of 'experiences' must be carefully designed to meet their sport-specific requirements as outlined in the Dual Continuum Classification Scheme of Officiating Role Demands.

Officiating requires ability, preparation, and experience. Without question, the first step in becoming an official is to gain a deep understanding of the rules or laws of the sport regardless of what that sport may be. However, to solely know the rules and the intent behind them is not enough. The second step, as outlined above, is to build on that knowledge through a gradual introduction to the perceptual-cognitive and movement demands of the competition environment. The use of simulated competition situations and shadowing of experienced officials – in an apprenticeship-like role – may be particularly effective in this regard. With patience, and appropriate investments in training to build their confidence and competence, officials will ultimately transition with success into officiating sport contests. However, the challenge for sport administrators in this regard is twofold. The first is to build effective training programs specific to the sport and officiating role in question. Most sport organizations offer some form of officiating training programs; however, such programs are rarely, if ever, evaluated to determine if they are actually effective in accomplishing their objectives. The second, and perhaps more challenging issue, is to resist the temptation to task a new official with overseeing a competition before they are ready.

TAKE AWAY MESSAGES FROM THIS CHAPTER

- The demands placed on an official are inheritably and inextricably associated with the nature and demands of the sport in which they are participating, as well as the specific role they are fulfilling during competition.
- Creating a classification scheme to understand the common elements experienced by all officials, as well as to capture both the complexity and the diversity of officiating tasks, is not an easy exercise.

The Dual Continuum Classification Scheme of Officiating Role Demands

- We have drawn from the work of others (Ellis, 1983; Plessner & MacMahon, 2013; Stefani, 1999) to create a Dual Continuum Classification Scheme of Officiating Role Demands. It acknowledges both the **extent of movement** and the **relative positioning of the official** outside, close to or moving in and out of, the competition area. The second continuum accounts for the **number of cues being monitored** while also **describing the environment and nature of play** as closed (or virtually unchanging) versus open (or constantly changing).
- Inserting each of the defined officiating roles for your sport within the dual continuum model will serve as a starting point for understanding the movement versus cognitive-perceptual demands associated with each and your choice of training approaches.

Training

- The training of every sport official begins with the acquisition of a full understanding of the rules, the intent behind the rules, and the technical aspects of rule application for their given sport.
- The second step in training is to build on rules knowledge through a gradual introduction to the perceptual-cognitive and movement demands of the competition environment.
- There are two current challenges faced by sports administrators responsible for the training of officials. The first is to build effective training programs specific to the sport and officiating role in question. Most sport organizations offer some form of officiating training programs; however, such programs are rarely, if ever, evaluated to determine if they are actually effective in accomplishing their objectives. The second, and perhaps more challenging issue, is to resist the temptation to task a new official with overseeing a competition before they are ready.

References

Clegg, R., & Thompson, W.A. (1985). *Sports officiating handbook*. Dubuque, IA: W.C. Brown Publishers.

Davis, K.L. (1996). *The art of sports officiating*. Boston, MA: Allyn & Bacon.

Green, B.C. (2005). Building sport programs to optimize athlete recruitment, retention, and transition: Toward a normative theory of sport development. *Journal of Sport Management, 19*, 233–253.

Hancock, D.J., Rix-Lièvre, G., & Côté, J. (2015). Citation network analysis of research on sport officials: A lack of interconnectivity. *International Review of Sport and Exercise Psychology, 8*(1), 95–105.

Hood, B. (1989). *Calling the shots: Memoirs of an NHL referee*. Toronto, Canada: General Publishing Company.

Korth, T. (2015). *Net gain: Officiating volleyball's tough calls*. Racine, WI: Referee Enterprises, Inc. and the National Association of Sports Officials (NASO).

Mackey, H.T., & Mackey, A.M. (1964). *Women's team sport officiating*. New York: Ronald Press Co.

MacMahon, C., Mascarenhas, D., Plessner, H., Pizzera, A., Oudejans, R., & Raab, M. (2014). *Sports officials and officiating: Science and practice*. London: Routledge.

McEvoy, H. (2002). *Horse show judging for beginners: Getting started as a horse show judge*. Guilford, CT: Lyons Press.

Pallone, D., & Steinberg, A. (1990). *Behind the mask: My double life in baseball*. New York: Penguin Books.

Pereira, M., & Jaffe, R. (2016). *After further review: My life including the infamous, controversial, and unforgettable calls that changed the NFL*. Chicago, IL: Triumph Books.

Plessner, H., & MacMahon, C. (2013). The sport official in research and practice. In D. Farrow, J. Baker, & C. MacMahon (Eds.), *Developing sport expertise: Researchers and coaches put theory into practice* (pp. 71–95). New York: Routledge.

Postema, P., & Wojciechowski, G. (1992). *You've got to have balls to make it in this league: My life as an umpire*. New York: Simon & Schuster.

Stefani, R.T. (1999). A taxonomy of sport rating systems. *IEEE Transactions on Systems, Man, and Cybernetics – Part A: Systems and Humans, 29*, 116–120.

Stern, J. (2002). *Smart football officiating*. Racine, WI: Referee Enterprises Inc.

Still, B. (2000). *101 tips for youth sports officials*. Racine, WI: Referee Enterprises Inc.

6 Valuing Sport Officials

Constructing the Optimal Officiating Environment

Sport is an important part of our social fabric and culture. It is not unusual for countries to identify a national sport or even to develop national pride around a sport in which they excel. In World Cup events, it is the norm rather than the exception to see crowds donning team colors and loudly rejoicing when their athletes are on the verge of defeating an opponent. Under these circumstances, the mood can be jovial whether the contest is taking place in a loud indoor arena setting or at an outdoor event beleaguered by rain. The volume and physical presence of spectators and the amount of noise they make will vary from contest to contest and venue to venue, as will the weather conditions and the quality of the playing environment. All of these factors help to define how challenging the physical environment (i.e., the structural venue, climatic conditions whether indoor or outdoor, and noise levels) may be when officials are performing their duties. At one end of the continuum, when the physical conditions are optimal (e.g., pristine state-of-the-art facilities, ideal weather, or playing conditions), the officiating experience may be a very positive one. On the other hand, when facilities are substandard and the weather or playing conditions are poor, officials' enjoyment levels and safety may be negatively compromised. Venue inspections conducted prior to competitions, enforcement of equipment and competition standards, and safety and weather-related policies can help to mitigate these worst-case scenarios. Less predictable and controllable, however, is the impact of athlete, coach, and spectator behavior on the overall officiating experience.

Just as the physical environment may vary, so too may the sociocultural environment or atmosphere surrounding a competitive match or competition. It is the product of multiple factors, some of which are defined prior to the contest (e.g., whether the competition is recreational or competitive in nature, a regular season versus playoff game or medal competition, the presence or absence of video replay, or taking place between two long-standing historic rivals) or at any given moment within it (e.g., the current score or standings, real or perceived bias, or errors in officiating). Experienced referees, umpires, and judges often welcome the opportunity to officiate under these high stakes circumstances, knowing that their years of preparation will assist them in responding to the dynamic environment associated with these competitions. This includes the critique which is sure to come from fans, athletes, and coaches. Preparation and experience are key to being able to perform well under these circumstances, but the question remains as to how best to support novice officials in preparing for and navigating these situations as they try to gain experience to endure such challenges?

The constraints and unpredictability of the sociocultural environment (both immediate and historical) surrounding sport is a complex issue. Indeed, sociocultural factors such as participation policies, overarching laws, and other public beliefs and socialized attitudes are various culturally driven, social constraints that shape and influence officials' practice environment and development (Dehghansai et al., under review). From what you have read in this book so far, you will know that sport officials perform their duties in an environment of constant critique. In an effort to mitigate this reality, sport organizations have used educational programs, behavioral contracts, and other mechanisms to try to monitor the verbal challenges and keep them in check. These efforts need to be continued, even though we know that they will never fully eliminate the possibility of an emotional or irrational player, coach, or fan acting out in inappropriate ways toward officials. Sport can bring out the best and worst in people and organizations cannot control the actions of all. However, they may create and, in effect, manage an environment for officials that offers positive supports to counterbalance the routine negativity associated with the officiating role.

Environmental constraints refer to the broader physical and social constructs, or perspectives, encountered while engaged in officiating, including, for example, the physical or natural environment (e.g., indoor or outdoor or large versus small venues), the immediate sociocultural environment (e.g., sport community), and the influence of fellow officials, friends, and other supporters (i.e., interpersonal environment constraints). Of primary and immediate impact on officials' participation and performance are infrastructure/organizational environmental constraints. This can include the organizational policies (e.g., governance structures, strategic plans, and remuneration and recognition) and practices (e.g., frequency of certification or recertification opportunities, mentorship programs, pay rates, recognition events) that underpin and influence officials' perceptions of the extent to which they are valued by a sport organization. We believe that those who understand the importance of creating a positive organizational environment for their officials will improve their success rates in recruiting, developing, retaining, and advancing officials through the ranks. It all comes down to a concept known as *perceived organizational support*, a crucial factor that differs among officials and requires further understanding to inform the design of desirable developmental climates for them to thrive in their challenging role.

Perceived Organizational Support (POS) and Participation Motivations

Emerging from the realm of the human resources and organizational behavior literature, Eisenberger and colleagues (1986) define perceived organizational support (POS) as a reflection of the degree to which an individual generally believes that an organization values their contributions, cares about their well-being, and is interested in fulfilling their socioemotional needs. Their theory of POS proposes that an individual's commitment to an organization is developed in response to what s/he perceives to be of benefit from either an economic (e.g., remuneration) or advancement (e.g., promotion) perspective. When an individual perceives that they are well supported by supervisors, being treated fairly, and rewarded for their efforts, POS is high. Conversely, when treatment is perceived to be unfair, support is seen to be lacking, and rewards are absent, POS is low. The key takeaway message here is that the likelihood of an individual committing to a role within an organization is positively or negatively influenced by high and low levels of POS, respectively. This is because POS is closely linked to and influences participation motivations and self-determination (Deci & Ryan, 1985).

Not everyone is motivated to become a sport official (Bernal, Nix, & Boatright, 2012), yet many do and the question as to why is important. Investigations have repeatedly found that individuals freely choose to enter sport officiating because they are intrinsically motivated by their love for the sport and their desire to remain connected to the social aspects of their sport community (Betts, Forbes, & Livingston, 2007; Hancock, Dawson, & Auger, 2015; Livingston & Forbes, 2016; 2017). This source of intrinsic motivation is developed for the majority through initial participation as an athlete and remains as a strong predictor of persistence in the role regardless of whether external incentives are present or absent (Betts et al., 2007; Hong, Jeong, & Downward, 2019; Livingston & Forbes, 2017). In contrast, remuneration as an extrinsic incentive may play a role in attracting some to officiate, but it does not appear to influence retention (Hancock et al., 2015). This is because intrinsic motivation is thought to be stimulated by the enjoyment officials experience while engaging in the activity itself (Brière, Vallerand, Blais, & Pelletier, 1995; Vallerand & Bissonnette, 1992). The motivations for continuing in sport officiating roles may also change over time to become less about why individuals entered into the activity to become more focused on what they hope to achieve through continued participation (e.g., a career pathway; Gjesdal, Appleton, & Ommundsen, 2017; Wagnsson, Lindwall, & Gustafsson, 2014).

For many, the camaraderie of peers and the resulting social networks found in sport provide sufficient motivation for persisting as officials (Livingston & Forbes, 2016), while others are motivated by the opportunity to excel to the highest ranks within their sport (Johansen, 2015).

This desire to advance to the highest levels is rooted in the basic human need for competence. In sport, competence is equated to performance, and for sport officials, performance is frequently evaluated and critiqued – rightly or wrongly – in the court of public opinion. While officials may learn to normalize such critique over time, perceptions of competence are most readily developed when meaningful feedback is provided by trusted supervisors and mentors. The provision of such feedback is important in establishing a supportive motivational climate to positively influence continued participation (Spencer-Cavaliere, Kingsley, & Gotwals, 2017). In contrast, when input from officiating supervisors is substandard or absent, effort and performance suffer, motivation to participate declines, and dropout may occur. This makes sense as all humans desire to have their contributions valued and respected by others. In an environment devoid of organizational support, where negative commentary from athletes, coaches, and spectators is the only form of feedback, this need is not met. Officiating organizations wishing to improve officials' retention and prolonged engagement in the activity must provide an environment that promotes positive beliefs and feelings of POS. Above and beyond the aforementioned need for constructive feedback from trusted mentors and supervisors, organizations must find ways to explicitly and implicitly support and value the participation of their officials in all facets of the organization.

Creating Supportive Officiating Environments

To create positive levels of POS for officials, everyone in your organization – sport administrators, paid employees, volunteers, and others – will need to continually invest time and effort into multiple activities. This is because there is no singular "magic bullet" or "fix" that will meet the needs or match the motivations of all of your referees, umpires, or judges. Their needs and motivations will also change over time; hence, there is a constant need for reinvestment and sensitivity to such fluctuating factors of officials' participation. The good news is that some of the following measures are inexpensive and easy to implement – these are the quick fixes. Other activities, in contrast, will require more effort and in some cases significant shifts in organizational culture. Organizational best practices, from our perspective, are those that support and meet the needs of officials by (a) recognizing them as key members of their organization by including them in organizational governance, planning, and policy-setting initiatives; (b) supporting them via the provision of high quality education, training, and mentorship programs; (c) adhering to clear and transparent policies and practices related to development and advancement opportunities, including competition assignments; (d) using simple common sense everyday practices; and (e) appreciating their efforts through both informal and formal forms of recognition.

In the following sections of this chapter, we will provide examples of various strategies in each of these categories. But, first, the next section aims to discuss governing and planning elements the organization should take into account when managing sport officiating development environments.

Organizational Governance, Plans, and Policies

Sport officials are all too often either a forgotten part of the sport eco-system or labelled as independent contractors – a designation that in-tentionally or unintentionally marginalizes or limits their participation. Through our research, we have come to understand that sport officials have a voice and they want to be heard. The reality, however, is that the structure of most sport organizations does not afford them opportuni-ties to participate in organizational governance or decision-making in meaningful ways. When organizations make decisions that affect offi-cials directly or indirectly, they should be part of the process (Hoye & Cuskelly, 2004; Sabaini, 2001). If they are excluded, they are left feeling devalued, unimportant, invisible, sometimes cynical, and often unmoti-vated to commit to the organization as a whole. Some effective strategies to counter these feelings and perceptions include the following:

- Ensure that your organization's governing body includes at least one officiating representative with voting privileges.
- Include officials in your organization's strategy and action plan setting meetings to ensure that their perspectives are heard and re-flected in the resulting documents. If you truly value your officials, you will identify objectives and goals to support their best interests as participants.
- Organizational policies and processes, and especially those which impact the officiating experience in any regard, should be developed with input from your officials.
- Elevate the profile of and value the role of officials within your or-ganization by ensuring that information about your governing body membership, planning documents, and policies – all of which ex-plicitly identify officiating representatives and officiating objectives and goals – are readily accessible and available to the general public. Web pages create a natural repository for such information.

Education, Training, and Mentorship Programs

We all can probably reflect back on our experiences in elementary or high school and quickly remember the best – and worst – teachers we ever had and the impact they had on our subsequent experiences and successes. The quality of instruction – the instructor's ability to capture the interest and imagination of their students and logically and clearly present the material – is just as important as presenting the material they need to know for success as an official. The basic rules or standards of performance, perhaps mixed with an introduction to the fundamental technical requirements of a given sport (e.g., correct positioning), are often the starting point for introductory officiating sessions. However, all too often this is the limit of their initial training, and novice officials are cast into the role of umpire, referee, or judge before they are ready. They are left to learn on the job and often without the requisite pre-competition training needed to develop confidence in their skills. The presence of an experienced supervisor or mentor in the early days of entry into officiating may help, but such supports tend to dwindle over time. A key piece of the puzzle in retaining and developing officials to the best of their potential requires effective education and training programs as well as clearly identified mentorship schemes. To this end, we suggest the following strategies:

- Find the best instructors – not just the most knowledgeable or experienced officials – to deliver your officiating clinics and educational programs. If needed, identify individuals with an understanding of the pedagogical principles underpinning effective instruction. For example, if you have a part-time or volunteer official who is employed as a teacher or college instructor, they may be able to fill this role effectively. If not, then commit to training your instructors and always gathering evaluations on their effectiveness from clinic participants.
- Develop a curriculum (i.e., the necessary topics or components), information manuals (e.g., situation manuals or case studies, in print or captured on video), and identify training goals (e.g., fitness levels) specific to your sport's needs. Ensure that all of your instructors consistently use these materials when delivering their classes and instructional clinics, as well as reinforce the importance of training goals.
- Ensure that your training curriculum includes information required by today's officials, not what you needed ten, twenty, or thirty years ago when you began your career. For example, consider including information on topics such as conflict management, effective communication techniques, and self-care, just to name a few.
- Annually evaluate the effectiveness of your organization's instructional efforts and revise your supporting materials (e.g., manuals and training videos), as necessary, accommodating the sport officials' task demands as dictated by the sport. Resist the temptation to only do this when there are rule changes within your sport.
- Consider using technology to ensure that all officials, regardless of location, have access to the most up-to-date training materials,

ideas, and qualified instructors. For example, cost-effective online and web-based platforms are now readily available and allow for live (or synchronous) delivery between locations.

- Formally schedule experienced officials, perhaps even some that may have retired due to the physical demands of the sport, to act as onsite mentors. Consider having mentors present at competitions, to work with officials during a match or even to debrief after the completion of a contest. In addition, provide opportunities for novice officials to connect with more experienced officials using email, teleconferencing, or videoconferencing technologies. These strategies, whether in-person or remote in nature, foster and contribute directly to a sense of community that often positively influences officials' POS.

- Promote continuous (or lifelong) learning and professional development for all of your officials, including those that have reached the highest levels of the sport and those transitioning out of sport.

Transparent Advancement Policies and Processes

The perception of fairness is exceptionally important in sport. Fairness applies to those who are officiating a contest (Mellick, Bull, Laugharne, & Fleming, 2005; Simmons, 2010, 2011) and to those responsible for evaluating officials' performances or assigning them to the championship match. Leventhal (1980) reported that perceptions of procedural fairness and organizational justice influence both an employee's performance and their commitment to the organization's mission. Further, when an individual feels unfairly treated by an "authority figure" responsible for guiding organizational activities, they ultimately view that authority as less competent, consistent, and accurate, and often reject their decisions and actions (Leventhal, 1980). Ultimately, diminished perceptions of fairness lead to greater uncertainty (Lind & Van den Bos, 2002).

All too often, the power and control evaluators and assignors possess is used to reward their friends or penalize those who do not abide with their wishes (Betts et al., 2007). When fairness is perceived to be lacking in these instances, the ability of an organization to retain officials is compromised. Cronyism is an age old problem in sport, and one that has affected some organizations and sports more than others. To effectively combat this, organizations must strive to make their policies and processes regarding advancement through the ranks, including game assignments, as transparent as possible (for further discussion on "Advancement" see Chapter 7). To this end, consider using the following strategies:

- Ensure that policies and processes related to the rating of officials (e.g., the criteria for advancement and evaluation rubrics) and contest assignments (e.g., minimal rating or prior experience requirements) are readily accessible and available to all that are interested in advancing through the ranks.

- When rating officials, have more than one individual complete the evaluation using a standardized evaluation rubric. The decision as to whether the individual reaches the next level should be the product of the combined scores received from the multiple assessors – and never based on a singular evaluation.

- If being fit is an important criterion for officials in your sport, institute standardized fitness testing, assessment protocols, and formalized reporting mechanisms for all officials.

- Officials, like athletes, are often intrinsically motivated to continually improve their performance. Given this, the opportunity for officials to rise through the ranks should never be thwarted by preset quotas or a real or perceived lack of available games or competitions to support those who qualify to work at a given level within the system. Instead, sport organizers should define alternate routes of excellence which will allow highly qualified individuals to work within the sport system. For example, while some will necessarily be assigned to competitions, others could play a role in supporting training pathways, mentorship programs, or other essential officiating tasks.

Simple, Common Sense Everyday Practices

When it comes to valuing people, the little things matter just as much as the big things. A simple "thanks for filling in at the last minute" or "I really appreciate the effort you put into your officiating" means more to people than you may ever imagine. If you cannot deliver the message in person, then a note or card, or even a quick supportive email will work. These small, common sense but also very overt strategies can make the difference as to whether someone stays or leaves an organization. Moreover, the ways officials are addressed in written or verbal communication – for example, when receiving constructive critique or learning of their lack of success in pursuing particular progression aspirations – have direct implications on the extent to which fair and just treatment is perceived. This is important as it is intrinsic to how officials perceive competence, accuracy, consistency, and accountability in organizational authorities and processes (Leventhal, 1980). Here are a few worthwhile strategies for you to consider and try:

- When hosting a game or competition, set aside a separate change room, meeting room, or space dedicated solely for use by the officials. If you can afford it, add fresh towels, bottles of water, or even some snacks.

- If it is within your organization's resources, ensure travel stipends or partial cost coverage is provided to officials to ensure they feel financially compensated.

- Younger officials really value getting a pay cheque in return for their officiating services, and often promptly. What seems like a minimal amount of money to you may seem like a lot of money to them. Regardless of the amount, set up a routine weekly, biweekly, or monthly pay schedule and stick to it. If you choose to go with the longer pay period, ensure that this is effectively communicated to the officials prior to the beginning of the season.
- Once a week, sit down and send 3–5 emails out to officials or other individuals within your organization, thanking them for helping you out with a task or for doing a good job.
- Assign individuals to be game or competition monitors, that is individuals who explicitly monitor the crowd for individuals who are heckling officials or being overly critical of their performance. Once identified, the monitor engages in a conversation to try and de-escalate the situation. Important note: Individuals assigned to be monitors need to be knowledgeable about the rules and the officiating role and effective communicators!

Informal and Formal Recognition Strategies

Human beings have an innate need to feel valued and respected by others. Saying thank you – as mentioned in the previous section – is one way to do this. Overt praise may also encourage and energize officials to continue during challenging times (Hancock, Dawson, & Auger, 2015). However, in sport, we routinely hand out awards to players for accomplishments and tend to do so with greater frequency than we might do with our officials. Recognition for a job well done can be a powerful extrinsic (or external) source of motivation. When officiating is perceived to be valued just as much as competing or coaching within your sport, the possibility of athletes transitioning into the role of official is enhanced. While some of these are simpler or more informal than others, consider using these strategies to recognize your officials:

- If your sport organization has a website, or if you issue a regular newsletter, add a column highlighting the "Official of the Month".
- At the conclusion of your competitive season, recognize officials on par with coaches and athletes via a formal awards program. For example, consider naming an "Official of the Year" or "Most Improved Official". Also, take time to recognize those who have experienced officiating milestones (e.g., being named to officiate at a major event or receiving an invite to an elite officiating training program or selection process).
- Offer small recognition scholarships to high school students who are about to set out and start a college- or university-level program.
- If your organization is situated in close proximity to a professional, semi-professional, or university- or college-based athletics program,

set up an annual recognition event which will take place during one of their competitions. Recognizing your top officials at half time during a soccer match or in between periods at a hockey game is doable!!

- If you are looking for a celebratory speaker to address athletes, coaches, and officials at your year-end awards banquet, ask an official to be your featured speaker.

Summary

With a little imagination, you can probably add a lot of your own ideas to this list. You know better than anyone what will work for your organization. Some of what we have suggested may or may not work for you and that is okay. The important thing, however, is to not dismiss what we have talked about in this chapter outright. You can always do something to value people, including your officials. Sports do it all the time for their athletes, coaches, and even their volunteers – so why not the officials? Your efforts will go a long way toward improving your retention rates in the officiating ranks.

TAKE AWAY MESSAGES FROM THIS CHAPTER

- The environment in which an official performs their duties consists of multiple physical and social constraints that influence their safety, well-being, and satisfaction.
- Sport officials perform their duties within an environment of critique. This is influenced by long standing historical biases, media reports, and ongoing real-time discussions on various media platforms.

Perceived Organizational Support (POS)

- Perceived organizational support refer to beliefs officials have about the degree their organization values their contributions, cares about their well-being, and is interested to make sure their socioemotional concerns are met.
- POS is linked to higher commitment to the officiating role and occupies an important role in retaining officials while they develop their skills.
- In reality, many officiating organizations provide minimal entry-level training for new officials. This leaves them feeling unprepared and needing to learn "on the job". This may hinder their ability to develop confidence in their officiating skills.

Inclusion of Officials in Organizational Governance and Training Opportunities

- Officials can sometimes feel disconnected from the organization's decision-making process, having little say and being afforded limited opportunities to participate in organizational governance in meaningful ways. Sport organizations need to allow for input from officials to acquire different perspectives and make officials feel like valued contributors to the structures directing their activity and participation.
- Opportunities for developing competencies and skills through task-appropriate and robust education, training, and mentorship – especially at the entry stages – are imperative to retaining and improving officials. Assess best suited individuals within the organization to lead training, seek outside expertise, develop comprehensive educational material, and find ways to increase official's experiences with mentors and other officials where resources and capacity provide this.

Showing Transparency and Giving Recognition

- Perceptions of fair process are instrumental to how consistently officials view superiors and authority figures to be competent and accurate in their assessments. Organizations must transparently articulate and demonstrate clear pathways for advancement. Conveying messages of fair process is integral to retain officials.
- Officials need to be recognized for their contributions. This can occur in multiple ways. The point being, when officials feel recognized and praised for the quality of duties they've carried out duties, or their volunteerism, they are more likely to continue in their role and be committed to their organization and their sport.

References

Bernal, J.C., Nix, C., & Boatright, D. (2012). Sport officials' longevity: Motivation and passion for sport. *International Journal of Sport Management, Recreation, & Tourism, 10,* 28–39. doi:10.5199/ijsmart-1791-874X-10b

Betts, M.J., Forbes, S.L., & Livingston, L.A. (2007). Factors contributing to the attrition of Canadian amateur ice hockey officials: The experiences of referees and linesmen in Atlantic Canada. *Avante, 11,* 15–22.

Brière, N.M., Vallerand, R.J., Blais, M.R., & Pelletier, L.G. (1995). Development and validation of a measure of intrinsic, extrinsic, and amotivation in sports: l'echelle de motivation dans les sports. *International Journal of Sport Psychology, 26,* 465–489.

Deci, E.L., & Ryan, R.M. (1985). The general causality orientations scale: Self-determination in personality. *Journal of Research in Personality, 19,* 109–134. doi:10.1016/0092-6566(85)90023-6

Dehghansai, N., Lemez, S., Wattie, N., Baker, J., & Pinder, R. (under review). Understanding the development of elite parasport athletes: Current understanding and future directions. *Frontiers in Psychology - Performance Science.*

Eisenberger, R., Huntington, R., Hutchison, S., & Sowa, D. (1986). Perceived organizational support. *Journal of Applied Psychology, 71,* 500–507. doi:10.1037/0021-9010.71.3.500

Gjesdal, S., Appleton, P.R., & Ommundsen, Y. (2017). Both the "what" and "why" of youth sports participation matter: A conditional process analysis. *Frontiers in Psychology, 8,* 659. doi:10.3389/fpsyg.2017.00659

Hancock, D.J., Dawson, D.J., & Auger, D. (2015). Why ref? Understanding sport officials' motivations to begin, continue, and quit. *Movement & Sport Sciences, 87,* 31–39. doi: 10.1051/sm/2014018

Hong, E., Jeong, Y., & Downward, P. (2019). Perceived organizational support, internal motivation, and work-family conflict among soccer referees. *Managing Sport and Leisure, 24,* 141–154. doi:10.1080/23750472.2019.1593049

Hoye, R., & Cuskelly, G. (2004). *Problems in recruiting and retaining sports officials: An exploratory study.* A report prepared for the Australian Sports Commission. Griffith University, Brisbane, Australia.

Johansen, B.T. (2015). Reasons for officiating soccer: The role of passion-based motivations among Norwegian elite and non-elite referees. *Movement & Sport Sciences, 87,* 23–30. doi:10.1051/sm/2014012

Leventhal, G.S. (1980). What should be done with equity theory? New approaches to the study of fairness in social relationships. In K. Gergen, M. Greenberg, & R. Willis (Eds.), *Social exchange: Advances in theory and research* (pp. 27–55). New York, Plenum Press.

Lind, E.A., & Van den Bos, K. (2002) When fairness works: Toward a general theory of uncertainty management. *Research in Organizational Behavior, 24,* 181–223.

Livingston, L.A., & Forbes, S.L. (2016). Factors contributing to the retention of Canadian amateur sport officials: Motivations, perceived organizational support, and resilience. *International Journal of Sports Science & Coaching, 11,* 342–355. doi:10.1177/1747954116644061

Livingston, L.A., & Forbes, S.L. (2017). Resilience, motivations for participation, and perceived organizational support amongst aesthetic sports officials. *Journal of Sport Behavior, 40,* 43–67.

Mellick, M., Bull, P., Laugharne, E., & Fleming, S. (2005). Identifying best practice for referee decision communication in association and rugby union football: A microanalytic approach. *Football Studies, 8,* 42–57.

Sabaini, D. (2001). *How to get and keep officials.* A special report published by the National Association of Sport Officials (NASO).

Simmons, P. (2010). Communicative displays as fairness heuristics: Strategic football referee communication. *Australian Journal of Communication, 37,* 75–94.

Simmons, P. (2011). Competent, dependable and respectful: Football 402 refereeing as a model for communicating fairness. *Ethical Space: The International Journal of Communication Ethics, 8,* 33–42.

Spencer-Cavaliere, N., Kingsley, B.C., & Gotwals, J.K. (2017). Ethic of care and the competitive ultimate Frisbee playing experiences of young women. *Leisure Studies, 36,* 329–340. doi:10.1080/02614367.2015.1105859

Vallerand, R.J., & Bissonnette, R. (1992). Intrinsic, extrinsic, and amotivational styles as predictors of behavior: A prospective study. *Journal of Personality, 60,* 599–620. doi:10.1111/j.1467-6494.1992.tb00922.x

Wagnsson, S., Lindwall, M., & Gustafsson, H. (2014). Participation in organized sport and self-esteem across adolescence: The mediating role of perceived sport competence. *Journal of Sport and Exercise Psychology, 36,* 584–594. doi:10.1123/jsep2013-0137

7 Developing and Implementing Officiating Development Plans/Programs

The purpose of this chapter is to describe a set of factors that can be considered when deciding how to develop and implement an officiating development plan or program (ODPs). Our goal at this point is to provide some structure, or rather provide some elements that may be useful to consider when planning ODPs, but also open up new understanding into how officiating development can be better conceived. In doing so, this chapter will present concepts and ideas from sport science research, as well as developmental theories and models.

Historically, the prevailing attitude with respect to the training and development of sport officials has been dominated by a short-term mindset. The inherent nature of the officiating participation, one influenced by attrition, turn-over, led by volunteers, and sometimes limited training resources, can lead to fragmented development experiences masked by more broad organizational goals of increasing officiating numbers to accommodate sport competitions (Titlebaum, Haberlin, & Titlebaum, 2009). Indeed, all too often, newly trained sport officials are thrown straight into competition with minimal training, and often after only completing a single training session or clinic (Forbes & Livingston, 2013). As a result, the role and caliber of sports officials has come under increased scrutiny over time. These systemic pressures highlight the importance of developing officials, referees, and umpires (Cuskelly, Evans, & Hoye, 2004; Kellett & Shilbury, 2007; Warner, Tingle, & Kellett, 2013). The pressures on athlete and coach development to ensure achieving the goals of sports organizations (e.g., podium appearances, medal counts) are being transferred to officiating practices. This emerging priority stems from governing bodies, with their emphasis on all stakeholders performing well (i.e., athletes, coaches, officials), and the sports who recognize the need for more dynamic and effective recruitment, retention, development, and support of sport officials (Adams, 2011; Forbes & Livingston, 2013; Sam, Andrew, & Gee, 2018). To address, and reformulate, this traditional short-term mindset to interpreting officials' development and planning, structuring support mechanisms should consider more expansive timelines prior to, during, and following officials' entry into and participation in sport.

Creating effective ODPs can also promote the value and positive experience that can be achieved by participating in sport as an official.

For example, officiating sports that have moderate to significant physical demands contributes to a healthy, active lifestyle. Physical activity is essential for overall health and well-being (Maher et al., 2013). However, in our country (Canada), the majority of children and adults routinely fail to meet the minimum guidelines for physical activity and sedentary behavior needed to experience benefits (e.g., 60 minutes of moderate to vigorous physical activity) (Colley et al., 2011). In addition to promoting physical benefits and a healthy lifestyle, officiating offers a societal role for fostering many other life skills and competencies, both relevant to sport and other occupations. For example, making accurate and rapid decisions that affect others, interacting with and managing those in other sport roles in pressure environments, organizing and planning, and other mental skills such as mental toughness, resilience, and emotional self-regulation represent attributes and experiences relevant to activities of daily living. Highlighting these factors as part of the processes and outcomes within ODPs, where appropriate, may help sport organizations advocate for the resources needed to promote and support officiating.

Using concepts and the understanding developed throughout Chapters 3–6, this chapter outlines some key components of planning and creating successful officiating development programs. Naturally, inter- and intra-sport variation in officials' developmental ecology (i.e., unique combinations of individual, environmental, and sport characteristics: Chapter 3) will inform the structure of ODPs. For example, *how do core competencies that define success in different sport officiating roles shape the principles and activities of a certain sport's ODP?* A 'time official' organizing the activities of other officials at a swim meet versus a North American football head referee versus a soccer assistant referee all have various role specificities that define their overarching priority competencies. Thus, when structuring an ODP, it may be important to consider what attributes related to an organization's officials' sport-specific task constraints serve as the basis of development programming aims and processes. In other words, role-specific competencies are two important areas to consider when planning an ODP. Furthermore, each organization needs to assess and understand its capacity to implement such a plan, meet mandates, and provide opportunities for all of their stakeholders (Misener & Doherty, 2009). Finally, and perhaps more importantly, one size does not fit all. What works for one sport may not work for another. And what works for one organization, even if it is in the same sport, may not work for others as a result of differences in organizational size and capacity (Nichols & James, 2008).

Developing an Impactful Officiating Development Program

Based on research, experience, and consultations, we have identified five (5) key components essential for setting up and implementing an effective ODP. The model presented in Figure 7.1 outlines the major components fundamental to a successful ODP. Underpinning this should be an evaluation plan of your organization's effort, which will be explored and discussed in Chapter 8. As the model depicts, development can be conceived as a central theme interconnected with other organizational activities related to managing official populations (recruit, entry, retain, advancement). As such, while we discuss components of the model independently, topics and components discussed are not mutually exclusive.

Recruitment

Recruitment is a complicated topic because of the many forms that it can take. *How* recruitment is done may depend on the characteristics of the officials and the unique characteristics of officials' sport-specific demands. In this section, we will highlight some of the different shapes that recruitment may take, and some considerations.

Recruitment Based on Convenience, Opportunity, and Incentive

Based on our own experiences, and conversations with practitioners, it is apparent that some sport officials are recruited by virtue of convenience. Often, these officials are recruited to participate because their children or grandchildren are participating as athletes. For example, at youth basketball games, it is not uncommon for an unsuspecting parent of

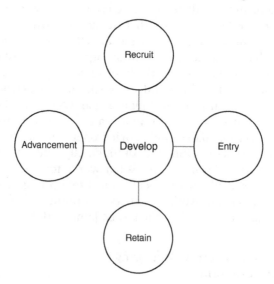

Figure 7.1 5-Factor process for officiating development.

an athlete to be recruited to score and time keep the match. From there word spreads that Parent X 'has done this before'. Similarly, anecdotes from track and field officials suggest they are similarly recruited by virtue of proximity. Some organizations, such as swimming clubs, require parents whose children participate in the sport to give back through various activities (e.g., fund raising, transportation, communication). Officiating presents another type of volunteer activity. While this may be a transient officiating population, organizations could consider efforts to retain these officials when their child is no longer involved (to be discussed below under Retention).

Some sports may wish to consider recruiting from older adult and former participant populations (coach and/or athlete). In Canada, approximately 43% of the population are older adults (5 million over 65 and 10 million between 45 and 64 years of age). By some estimates, this group contributes more than one billion volunteering hours a year (see Cook & Sladowski, 2013). For example, several track and field organizations in Ontario recruit their officials from local 55+ groups (Livingston & Forbes, 2016). Emphasizing social connection can be an important recruiting tool for this population. However, older adult populations have high expectations for their volunteering experiences. They may want social connections and meaningful opportunities to contribute to their communities, but may also be looking for opportunities to develop new skills (see Cook & Sladowski, 2013). These factors, as well as barriers like transportation and out-of-pocket costs, need to be considered when structuring entry and developmental experiences.

It may also be possible to use incentives to recruit officials. Some sports have the capacity to pay officials. This is particularly attractive to younger individuals who see this as a viable source of income. Money as a recruitment tool works to get the budding official "in the door"; however, this extrinsic motivator can drop off when remuneration is mishandled (e.g., delayed payments), and officials recognize they can gain income through other means, perhaps with less stress and uncertainty (Betts, Forbes, & Livingston, 2007).

Organizations could also consider other incentives to facilitate recruitment (and retention). For example, if officials wish to also participate in their sport as an athlete, they could be eligible for reduced registration/league fees, or discounts on apparel and equipment from community sponsors. Organizations can also pursue creative incentives. One possibility is that organizations with chartable status may be able to devise a system where officiating is considered a form of charitable donation, eligible for tax receipts. Importantly, while incentives may facilitate recruitment, they may also signal to officials how much their organization values and supports them. Certainly, not all sports and organizations have the capacity and resources to incentivize officials.

Athlete-to-Official Recruitment

Research has shown that 80–90% of active officials started and/or are participants in the sport they officiate (Cuskelly & Hoye, 2013; Livingston & Forbes, 2016). Many see officiating as a way to "give back" and/or continue their involvement in the sport they love (Hancock, Dawson, & Auger, 2015). Some also see this as an opportunity to build on existing skills (see Chapters 4 and 6 for more on motivation). Additionally, this is a group that is familiar with their sport and can bring a level of knowledge/expertise with respect to formal rules and to the nuances and inner workings of that sport (Livingston & Forbes, 2016). Indeed, in studies of expertise development, officials report that prior participation in sport as athletes was an important influence on their *development* (Mack, Schulenkorf, Adair, & Bennie, 2018; Ollis, Macpherson, & Collins, 2006). The challenge for sport organizations is to consider what skills prior participation as an athlete develop, and *how* they want to recruit athletes into officiating roles.

One method simply involves *awareness raising* and *self-selection*. For example, organizations can raise awareness about officiating by actually exposing athletes and coaches to what's involved. For example, recently a soccer/football club in Ontario mandated attendance at an officials' clinic for both players and coaches. While the initial intent of the directive was to educate those individuals about the requirements, responsibility, and role of officials, an unanticipated outcome was that it attracted players and/or coaches to the officiating ranks at a later date (i.e., athletes self-selected to become an official[1]). The benefits of this approach are that it may have ancillary benefits (e.g., increasing respect for officials), and it probably involves relatively minimal resources to implement. For sports and organizations that have significant attrition problems and challenges meeting demands to supply officials, this approach may be promising. However, this approach exerts a relatively low level of control over *who* is recruited, which may have implications for the quality officials' involvement and dedication.

Organization can also recruit officials more purposefully from athlete populations. This approach would be akin to existing athlete *talent identification* initiatives (see Robinson, Wattie, Schorer, & Baker, 2018). In this case, those wishing to identify talented officials would explicitly search an athlete population for people they see as having potential. This can be done more informally by encouraging coaches and current officials to identify athletes that they feel have potential to be good or great officials, and perhaps have them provide those athletes with resources on how to become involved as an official. Alternatively, talent identification can be more formally carried out, with sport organizations taking structured approaches to talent identification. Central to talent identification is that there are characteristics (see Chapter 4) that can be identified, which reflect the future potential of a prospective official. To our knowledge, the body of literature on talent identification of officials is extremely limited compared to what exists for athletes. However, parallels can be drawn from the research on athletes, and some useful lessons applied to ODPs.

Perhaps, the main lesson from the athlete literature is that talent identification is fraught with complexity and limitations (see Baker, Cobley, Schorer, & Wattie, 2017). First, there are no clear and agreed upon definition of what talent actually is, certainly none that have much utility to practitioners (see Baker, Wattie, & Schorer, 2019). Second, even if some agree that innate talent exists (Simonton, 2017), the concept has limited real-world use (Baker & Wattie, 2019). In particular, there are numerous issues related to the accuracy of talent identification programs (see Abbott, Button, Pepping, & Collins, 2005; Baker, Schorer, & Wattie, 2018). Also, talent identification typically has very low levels of predictive accuracy (Koz, Fraser-Thomas, & Baker, 2012; Robinson et al., 2018). These low levels of accuracy often result from common errors and biases in talent identification. For example, confusing talent and performance is a common error (Abbott et al., 2005).[2] Practitioners should also be cautious of making talent selection decisions based on one discrete snapshot of performance and/or based on one component of officiating performance. Talent, like officiating performance, is multidimensional (Baker et al., 2019; Mascarenhas, Collins, & Mortimer, 2005), and research suggests that when multiple characteristics are measured (e.g., physical, psychological, cognitive, and affective), accuracy of talent identification increases (Robinson et al., 2018). To facilitate talent identification evaluation (see Chapter 8), it is important for organizations to specify what the criteria are for successful talent identification. Is a talent identification initiative successful if it has a 5% or 20% success rate? Each organization has to decide what is their goal or criteria for success.

Tips:

1   Recruit from within by seeking out athletes, coaches, and/or parent volunteers.
2   Reach out to your community by looking for people seeking ways to give back and be engaged with others in the community.
3   How would you describe what officiating talent "is" in your sport?

Entry into Officiating

This component of planning ODPs relates to what organizations provide to officials once they are recruited, particularly during early stages of participation. Previous research found that officials, regardless of age or years of experience, commented on the poor quality of training they received. Additionally, studies found that about 85% of respondents felt their organization regularly offered clinics, while only 73% said they offered more than one a year. Also, regularly scheduled clinics are more likely designed for the entry-level official (Auger et al., 2010; Livingston & Forbes, 2007). In a recent survey, only 61% thought the clinics offered by their sport were of high quality, while about a third questioned the quality of their clinics (Forbes, Livingston, & Thevakumar, 2018).

One of the factors that influence motivation, continued participation, and progression to different stages of participation is self-efficacy. As described in Chapter 4, self-efficacy is a person's perceptions of their capabilities to successfully organize and execute courses of action to produce specific outcomes (Bandura, 1997). For officiating, this includes game knowledge, decision-making, coping with pressure/stress, communication (Myers, Feltz, Guillén, & Dithurbide, 2012), and fitness and positioning. Importantly, we know from the sport and exercise psychology literature that self-efficacy is lower at early stages of participation (see Mack, Sabiston, McDonough, Wilson, & Paskevich, 2016 for a summary). The fact that officials are thrown into their roles quickly and with relative little preparation likely reinforces the importance of targeting self-efficacy support during early phases of participation.

One of the benefits of focusing on self-efficacy during entry into officiating is that there are concrete ways to increase self-efficacy; specifically, through reinforcing past performance success, vicarious experience, physiological/affective experiences, and social persuasion; Myers et al., 2012). Experience level (past performance) is an important correlate of self-efficacy. More experience (and success) results in higher levels of self-efficacy. While self-efficacy and past experience distinguish officials of different levels of expertise (and therefore may take time to develop), organizations can try to provide consistent opportunities and/or provide tangible feedback about performances early during participation. Perhaps most importantly, physical and mental preparation has been identified as having a significant and positive impact on all elements of officiating self-efficacy (Myers et al., 2012). Providing tools, checklists, and training resources can help to increase entry-level officials' perceptions of their physical and mental preparedness as well as their confidence in their abilities to perform. Another way to increase self-efficacy is by trying to improve the physiological and affective experiences of entry-level sport officials. Myers et al. (2012) describe this as 'environmental comfort'. Increasing respect for officials within sport culture and modifying the environmental characteristics (e.g., proximity to spectators) may help to decrease the negative physiological and affective (e.g., stress and anxiety) experiences of entry-level officials.

Interestingly, research has not reported a link between social support and officiating self-efficacy. This may simply be due to the absence of social support, however, not the absence of an influence of social support on self-efficacy. Organizations may wish to consider mentorship programs for entry-level officials to increase the influence of social persuasion and social support on self-efficacy levels.

Consideration must essentially also be given to:

- The quality of the clinic(s) being offered: Are they relevant to the level of the cohort being trained?
- Are the clinics effectively evaluated from several perspectives (e.g., participant, practitioner, third party)?
- Are your clinic materials current? How often are they updated? We recently found that only 2/3rds felt their materials were up to date? (Forbes, Livingston, & Thevakumar, 2018).
- Are the clinics supported by relevant resources, such as online resources, stress management, conflict resolution (whether developed in-house or via external links), mentorship opportunities, etc.?
- Does your organization lever technology effectively to support officiating training? For example, online exams, situation videos.

Tips:

1 Focus on "what" is provided to officials once they're recruited them.
2 Include information on clinics (e.g., quality, frequency).
3 Use and availability of resources.
4 Leverage technology.
5 Provide practice opportunities.

Retain

The unfortunate historical record of participation and dropout trends suggests that some sport's ODPs may need to explicitly consider strategies to retain sport officials. In the United States, the National Association of Sport Officials (NASO) gathered high-profile sports officials and sport managers to discuss official retention issues in sport. One theme raised for discussion concerned possible overlaps between sport officials and industry and business management (where an organizational aim is to retain employees) in ways to treat officials' retention. A set of retention initiatives were recommended, including (i) increase professionalization in the sport association (i.e., objective systems, formal performance evaluation); (ii) involve officials/others in the decision-making process (i.e., integrate new ideas/opinions and construct balance between authority and accountability), (iii) help officials acquire new skills (e.g., access to training tools and modalities, access to expert knowledge from within and outside sport, quantity and quality of workshops/clinics), and finally, (iv) institute "welfare measures" (i.e., heighten awareness and accommodation to officials' life and other time and effort commitments; Sabaini, 2001). While concepts used with job employees could prove effective to the officiating world, today's officiating population may require a tailored approach that considers their own sport's retention trends/dynamics and evolved sporting climate officials participate.

In sport, one fact that organizations may need to consider is that different types of officials may have unique preferences about how they want to be recognized. For example, research suggests that "monitor" officials were more concerned with receiving recognition from within the organization (praise), while "interactors" were affected by respect from participants (coaches, parents, players) (Hancock, Dawson, & Auger, 2015). Other recommendations for *why* officials continue emphasize reinforcing comradery, enjoyment, dedication, and advancement among officials (Fowler, Smith, Nordstrom, Ferguson, 2019).

One factor that may influence retention is officials' perception of organizational support (POS). As discussed in detail in the previous chapter, POS is the degree to which officials believe their organization values their contributions and cares about their well-being and fulfills their role-related needs (Livingston & Forbes, 2016). When officials have higher POS, they demonstrate intrinsic motivation (e.g., driven by internal rewards) in their role (Hong, Jeong, & Downward, 2019). POS is seen as an organization's contribution to a positive reciprocity (i.e., the practice of exchanging things with others for mutual benefit) dynamic with sports participants, in this case officials, as these individuals tend to perform better to reciprocate received rewards and favorable treatment. Also critical to this is *clarity* and *transparency* in those interactions. From a retention perspective, POS can be achieved through several means:

- Providing awards that recognize their contribution to the sport/ organization.
- Establishing clear policies and procedures with respect to advancement.
- Evaluating objectively.
- Providing formal/structural recognition within the sport organization (e.g., Representation on the Board, Officials Committee)
- Investing in human resources.
- Facilitating inclusion in the relevant decision-making process.
- Increasing organizational commitment to officiating development.

Tips:

1   Focus on "how" to keep officials (for useful resources see Sabaini, 2001; Titlebaum, Haberlin, & Titlebaum, 2009).

2 Introduce the POS concept and emphasize its value.
3 Include information related to formal recognition, inclusion, policies, and procedures.
4 Emphasize the need for transparency, objectivity, investment, and commitment.

Develop

Naturally, ODPs need to include considerable emphases on development. This element is arguably underdeveloped and misconceptualized in sport management models. Moreover, those tasked with creating development plans in sport predominately focus on skill and ability development, and pathways, not human resource management principles or sport development (though these components are important). This is why we place *develop* at the center of the model (see Figure 7.1) in this chapter. In this section, we will highlight what we feel are important elements to consider when structuring ODPs. Specifically, we discuss macro and micro structures of practice and learning (i.e., specific and broad complexities in optimal performance environments), as well as useful elements of existing developmental models from the sport science literature.

Developmental Complexity: Macro and Micro Structures of Practice and Learning

Development is complex and multidimensional. Here, we try to introduce concepts critical to the way we should envision and, ultimately, approach developing and improving officials. An important distinction is the "macro" and "micro"[3] characteristics of officiating development. Macro structures of practice and learning refer to broader histories and total volumes of participation and training (Davids, Güllich, Shuttleworth, & Araújo, 2017; Farrow, Reid, Buszard, & Kovalchik, 2018; Güllich, 2019). This category within developmental models includes factors such as age of entry into officiating, total accumulated hours of officiating-specific training/practice, and total hours spent officiating competitions. At a very basic level, these developmental data help us to understand who officials are and where they come from. For example, MacMahon and colleagues observed that elite soccer referees (on the FIFA list of referees) had a younger average start age than non-elite referees (non-FIFA): 18.1 years versus 21.4 years, respectively (MacMahon, Helsen, Starkes, & Weston, 2007).

Gathering data about macro developmental features may also be useful for understanding different officiating roles within a sport. For example, highly skilled Belgian soccer referees are shown to have younger average debut ages (17.9 years) than assistant referees (19.1 years) (Catteeuw, Helsen, Gilis, & Wagemans, 2009). Interestingly, the assistant referees had reported that they began their careers as referee (accumulating approximately 15 years of experience), before deciding to become an assistant referee. Understanding milestones, such as debut age, can help to understand factors that influence development. They can serve as proxies for motivation and interest (and, therefore, may be useful for talent identification). They also help to understand, broadly, how much time, and experience is needed to reach different levels of officiating (which is essential to structuring training and development plans, as well as ODP pathways).

From a developmental standpoint, macro data help to distinguish performers of different skill level. They highlight how those that achieve different levels of expertise may have unique and identifiable milestones, benchmarks for accumulated training, and/or match officiating experience. These can be used for both talent identification and development initiatives. Arguably, the topic most discussed and debated within this realm is deliberate practice. Deliberate practice is used to improve skill/ performance and is generally described as something needing effort (i.e., requiring high energy and attention) from an individual/learner, and thus feels unpleasant or unenjoyable to do (Ericsson, Krampe, & Tesch-Römer, 1993). While considerable debate exists about the specific role and nature of practice (Baker & Young, 2014; Ericsson & Harwell, 2019; Ericsson et al., 1993; Hambrick, Burgoyne, Macnamara, & Ullén, 2018; Hambrick et al., 2014; Macnamara, Hambrick, & Oswald, 2014),[4] there is no doubt that total practice/training (in hours and years) is one of the primary influences on expertise development (Baker & Horton, 2004), and an important distinguisher of different expertise levels. For example, the study by Catteeuw et al. (2009) found significant differences in officiating skill (i.e., between those that had achieved national versus international levels of expertise) in terms of total years officiating, accumulated practice hours, practice hours per week, and the overall number of accumulated matches officiated. As such, understanding macro factors (like total practice and match officiating hours accumulated) is likely important to understand differences in performance at all levels of officiating.

Generally speaking, very little is known about how macro factors influence the development of sport officials. To this end, most of the few studies available (see Catteeuw et al., 2009; MacMahon et al., 2007) focus on elite officials, but little understanding is known about different levels of officiating (i.e., from grassroots toward elite pathways). Knowing how these factors influence development of sport officials can help to establish guidelines, goals and areas for improvement (i.e., increased training), and pathways for ODPs. Macro structures have been essential in informing developmental models for athlete development (see Côté, Baker & Abernethy, 2007; Côté & Fraser-Thomas, 2016; Gulbin, Croser, Morley & Weissensteiner, 2013). Going forward, as organizations map their ODPs they will need to consider their sp*ort-specific* macro training and participation profiles related to performance and expertise development. From a research perspective, there is much to be done in this area.

Micro structures of practice refer to the *specific* activities related to participation and training in sport (Davids et al., 2017; Farrow et al., 2018; Güllich, 2019). For example, while macro training may refer to overall number of hours practiced, micro training refers to the specific types (and amounts) of practice. Both Catteuw et al. (2009) and Mac-Mahon et al. (2007) excellently present the breadth of micro practice and participation types for soccer referees. For example, micro practice and participation activities in their studies included on-field practice (e.g., high, low and recovery runs, agility training, and technical abilities), off-field practice (e.g., strength training, video analysis, and psychological skills training), therapeutic/recovery activities (e.g., physiotherapy), match-related activities (e.g., referring league versus exhibition games), coach/playing activities (e.g., playing organized soccer, reading about soccer, travel, and meetings), and everyday life activities (e.g., sleep and leisure). The Cornerstones model also highlights specific micro areas for training and performance (see Mascarenhas, Collins, & Mortimer, 2005). Again, understanding these micro activities can provide insights into the participation and training activities that influence development. For example, research suggests that match-referring experience (i.e., amount of actual match-refereeing) may be the most important (relevant) micro activity for skill development (Catteew et al., 2009; MacMahon et al., 2007).

When combined, macro and micro profiles of sport-specific officiating developmental activities can be incorporated into ODPs to structure the amount and type of training at specific stages of participation/development, and to outline the different developmental pathways for officials. Naturally, there is likely to be significant inter-sport variation in this structure. While expertise development has been a focus of this section, and the literature, it will be important for pathways and development structures (macro and micro) to optimize development at each level of participation, regardless of whether an official has the desire or capability to progress to a higher level of officiating. As such, central to optimizing ODPs is a clear vision for what 'optimal performance' looks like at each level of officiating, and a sound plan for how to support development and performance accordingly.

Stages and Phases of Development

Given the limited research on officials' development (Pina, Passos, Araújo, & Maynard, 2018), we hesitate to put forward a specific developmental model or to advocate for the use of an existing developmental model. Certainly, however, there are a number of existing models that can be used to inform initial steps of ODPs. A detailed review of athlete development models, and of general models of expertise, is beyond the scope of this chapter (see Baker & Wattie, in press; Hambrick et al., 2018). Nevertheless, there are some promising recommendations that can be made based on what exists.

Perhaps, the most relevant and available model that can be used to inform ODPs is the Foundation, Talent, Elite and Mastery (FTEM) conceptualization, which was designed to create and optimize developmental pathways for athletes (see Gulbin et al., 2013). MacMahon et al. (2015) also suggest that this is a promising model to inform ODPs. The FTEM is a stage-based model that describes four primary stages (which also contain sub-stages). The first stage, *Foundation*, generally emphasizes fundamental elements. For officiating this may include, but not limited to, establishing and developing foundational levels of fitness, coordination, and knowledge of the rules. Importantly, this stage would involve early exposure to officiating training and experiences. As officials progress through the Foundation sub-stages, there is generally an increase in training and engagement, and differences in motivation and commitment have emerged. For most officials, Foundation would likely begin and take place at grassroots recreational levels and involve increased practice hours and diversification of training activities. In the *Talent* stage, there is an increased focus on developing the qualities and attributes associated with high performance officiating. It is during this stage where selection (talent identification and development) and training would become more targeted and formal. Research on athletes suggests that toward the end of this stage performers seek out the highest levels of support for continued development. By the end of this stage, the certification and performance requirements that have to be met become much more stringent. Those at the *Elite* stage have officiated at national and/or international levels, while those at the *Mastery* stage have demonstrated repeated exceptional performance at the highest levels of their sport.

While the FTEM is not a "perfect" representation of officials' development, or possibly relevant to all sports (but adaptable), what it does provide is a useful map for informing initial stages of an ODP by conceptualizing development periods (related to participation and promotion). This model can aid in identifying relevant skills and performance focus that can color learning emphasis depending on the officiating level you support. First, the FTEM stages are as intuitively relevant to officiating as athletes (the levels of sport and performance are the same for both). It also considers both the development of skills and abilities, as well as performance. This helps ground the FTEM in more practical and ecological ways than many other models. Second, it is informed by research and practitioners. Some models, such as the Long-Term Athlete Development (LTAD) model, are not evidence based, have not been supported by research, and should be used and applied cautiously when designing ODPs (Baker &

Wattie, in press; Ford et al., 2011). Third, the FTEM is non-linear. It acknowledges that performers can skip stages, enter and exit officiating at different levels, and/or not progress through stages in a linear fashion (how long a performer stays at a stage is not prescribed, and they can go backward). These features are consistent with reports of officials' developmental trajectories, which are described as non-linear (Ollis et al., 2006). Third, the FTEM is more flexible than models such as the Developmental Model of Sport Participation (Côté et al., 2007; Côté & Fraser-Thomas, 2016), which are so specific to athlete development that it would be difficult to adapt for officials. This flexibility makes it possible to acknowledge role and influence of prior participation (macro and micro) as an athlete to development. While more detail is needed about the nature of prior/current athlete participation (i.e., duration and level of participation as an athlete), research on officials reinforces this an important element of ODPs.

Crucially, the FTEM includes macro and micro elements of training *and* participation and acknowledges both as important for development. It is but one model, but a useful one, and should be interpreted carefully when addressing your sport's officials. This is also consistent with evidence on officials' development. For example, the theory of deliberate practice, and the deliberate practice framework, is likely not multidimensional enough to be the sole framework for designing ODPs. The importance of match-officiating experience for expertise development is not consistent with the deliberate practice framework (Catteeuw et al., 2009; MacMahon et al., 2007).

- What are the macro participation and training profiles of your officials (and officials of different levels within your organization)?
- What are the specific micro participation and training activities that apply to your sport?
- How do macro and micro participation and training profiles change at different levels of officiating?

Advancement and Thriving

Opportunity for advancement occupies one relevant factor in why officials exit (i.e., lack thereof of opportunity; Forbes & Livingston, 2013) and continue in their sport (Fowler et al., 2019). Officials can be just as competitive as athletes, and should have available development pathways or routes that allow for challenge and build self-efficacy (Myers et al., 2012). When officials can anticipate pathways for progression, often this encourages self-determination (Deci & Ryan, 1985) and intrinsic motivation can be enhanced. Not all officials may want to progress, but development programs should plan ways skill development-challenge tradeoff is treated within officials' promotion and participation to ensure they thrive in their sport. "Advancement" can be as arbitrary as officials being given opportunity to move into other adjudication roles in their sport (e.g., after gaining experience as a linesman/assistant, to then be granted central official responsibilities) to being appointed to the 'big match' and other nomination to appointment to international, national, or regional competitions and tournaments (Fowler et al., 2019). Also, considering athletes need organizational support to help guide ways they *advance out of sport*, only until recently have officiating scholars questioned best ways to formalize strategies to help officials transition from sport (MacMahon & Rix-Lièvre, 2019).

To foster officials' attitudes that opportunities to advance exist for them (while being realistic that not all officials should be allowed to advance), a combination of two (2) critical factors are worth highlighting: *Individual desire* and *capability*. First, and as previously noted, not all officials desire or want to move up their sport's officiating ranks. Many officials, for their own reasons, are comfortable working at the lower levels (e.g., community-based because kids involved in the sport), or otherwise don't foresee clearly marked advancement pathways and/or fairly evaluated processes due to perceived political or organizational climate within their sport association. Second, *capability* refers to the ability to perform or achieve certain actions or outcomes. When thinking about development, as it applies to officiating, we're really talking about the intersection of capacity and ability. To assess an official's readiness to "advance", outlined below are some important considerations:

- Physical ability and knowledge competencies: Do they understand the rules, including interpretation, sufficiently to operate at the next level AND are they physically up for the job (e.g., fitness level)?
- Do they have sufficient self-regulation skills, or emotional intelligence (see Chapter 4; individual constraints), to operate at the next level?
- Advancement process is clearly communicated, transparent, and open to all qualified individuals.
- Level of commitment and passion for officiating.

Organizations can allow advancement of capability to progress through a natural or targeted processes. In more natural or organic systems, developmental resources (training and education) are provided and the cream is allowed to rise to the top. In this case, those that have the motivation, commitment, skill, best performance, and/or resilience to advance to higher levels. In some ways this is the system described by the differentiated model of giftedness and talent (DMGT: Gagné, 2004), where the top 10% of performers (in terms of natural abilities and developed skills) are allowed to progress to higher levels through a process of selective cuts. This approach is limited by the fact that individuals often do not follow a linear developmental path (Gulbin et al., 2013; Ollis et al., 2006), and that performance at one level/developmental stage generally does not correlate with performance at the next level/developmental stage. Another way of structuring advancement is to conduct talent identification searches.

Advanced development (beyond entry-level clinics) opportunities can include:

- Clearly defined officiating development pathways/objectives.
- Training opportunities at advanced levels (e.g., "Friendlies").
- Advanced-level seminars.
- Multi-level Certification programs (e.g., Speedskating Canada has a 5-level certification program).
- Standardized examinations (written and observational). These should be well communicated and the evaluation criteria transparent.
- Talent identification programs (e.g., Ontario Soccer's Long Term Officials Development (LTOD) program).
- Pursuing additional accreditation based on international standards (i.e., Rugby Canada's officiating accreditation provided by the International Rugby Board).
- Official-specific meetings/conventions (e.g., Softball Canada's Blue Convention).
- These cohort-specific gatherings provide an officiating community an opportunity.
- to build a sense of belonging, as well as allowing officials to work collectively to improve their skills and discuss common issues.
- Engagement of more experienced officials in mentorship programs.
- Provide them opportunities to help develop relevant resources (e.g., training material, training scenarios).
- Provide relevant resources. These can include officials' handbooks that contain all relevant policies, development/pathway model, assessment forms, etc.

Summary

Many, if not most, organizations tend to concentrate efforts on recruiting new officials to their sport with limited attention to working with those who are already in the system. While a certain amount of attrition is inevitable and the need to replace those who leave, working to retain and support continuing officials is vital to the success of the organization. Focusing on the latter group enables an organization to improve the quality of sport experience for all participants (e.g., athletes, coaches, spectators) while ensuring that talent and expertise develop over time is sustained. Additionally, the remaining officials provide additional development resources for new officials (e.g., mentors). The model presented in this chapter provides guidelines for getting officials into the system and sustaining them throughout their career path. Key to this undertaking is understanding what your organization is capable of and that it is unique based on that. Finally, critical to sustaining officials is ensuring their training is relevant to their level, that advancement opportunity is one option within officiating development programs, and that they are seen as a valued member of your sport community.

TAKE AWAY MESSAGES FROM THIS CHAPTER

Plan

Take careful steps to organize processes you will implement and types of relevant factors you wish to consider in your officiating development plan (ODP).

Recruit

Look within the sport for athletes, coaches, and/or parent volunteers, particularly those who want to give back to their sport. Consider recruiting for talent, and what officiating talents are worth considering when recruiting.

Entry into Sport

Once recruited, focus on what is provided to officials in terms of educational and training sports through use of technology platforms, practice opportunities, and quality of resources.

Retention

Emphasize developmental climates that foster perceived organizational support for sport officials. This can be facilitated through increased transparency, displays of professionalism, addressing officials' socioemotional and welfare needs, and including them within decision-making processes.

Development

Consider if/how differences in participation histories (e.g., what age participants start officiating, how many years they have officiated, and how many match-hours of officiating they engage in across time) influence developmental and performance differences among your officials.

Consider which specific practice activities (e.g., knowledge of rules, physical conditioning training, interaction, and game management training) should be focused on at different developmental stages (Foundation, Talent, Elite or Mastery) of officiating in your sport.

Together, participation histories and specific practice activities can be combined to structure and plan sport-specific ODPs.

Advancement and Ongoing Support

Consider the interest for advancement within the officiating system that some officials strive for that keep them in the sport. Creating challenging learning opportunities and awareness to officials' individual desire and capability should also be considered.

Notes

1 We have also encountered some sports (i.e., squash) that *requires* participating athletes to officiate at tournaments they attend, in matches that they are not taking part in.
2 It is also important to be aware of differences between innate talent and expertise. Where innate talent describes potential that results at least partially from genetic characteristics, expertise refers to exceptional and consistent superior performance. Talent is an antecedent of expertise (see Baker et al., 2019).
3 Macro refers to higher-order (or low-fidelity) factors of officials' practice and learning (i.e., development histories, deliberate practice hours), while micro refers to more detailed and fine elements (immediate, day-to-day training activities and experiences).
4 There are a number debates about (i) what deliberate actually is (what counts as deliberate practice and what does not), and (ii) how important accumulated deliberate practice is for skill formation and expertise development. This is a very complicated topic that warrants more discussion than this chapter permits, but readers should be critical of the oversimplified and inaccurate discussions of deliberate practice in popular books like *Outliers* (Gladwell, 2008) or *Bounce* (Syed, 2010). Moreover, there are elements of the deliberate practice framework that may not be generalizable to officiating development.

References

Abbott, A., Button, C., Pepping, G-J., & Collins, D. (2005). Unnatural selection: Talent identification and development in sport. *Nonlinear Dynamics, Psychology, and Life Sciences, 9*, 61–88.

Adams, A. (2011). Between modernization and mutual aid: The changing perceptions of voluntary sports clubs in England. *International Journal of Sport Policy and Politics, 3*(1), 23–43.

Auger, D., Fortier, J., Thibault, A., Magny, D., & Gravelle, F. (2010). Characteristics and motivations of sports officials in the province of Québec. *International Journal of Sport Management Recreation & Tourism*, 5(b), 29–50.

Baker, J., Cobley, S., Schorer, J., & Wattie, N. (Eds.). (2017). *The Routledge handbook of talent identification and development in sport*. London: Routledge.

Baker, J., & Horton, S. (2004). A review of primary and secondary influences on sport expertise. *High Ability Studies, 15*, 211–228.

Baker, J., Schorer, J., & Wattie, N. (2018). Compromising talent: Issues in identifying and selecting talent in sport. *Quest, 70*, 48–63 doi:10.1080/00336297.2017.1333438

Baker, J., Wattie, N., & Schorer, J. (2019). A proposed conceptualization of talent in sport: The first step in a long and winding road. *Psychology of Sport & Exercise, 43*, 27–33.

Baker, J., & Young, B. (2014). 20 years later: deliberate practice and the development of expertise in sport. *International Review of Sport and Exercise Psychology, 7*(1), 135–157.

Bandura, A. (1997). *Self-efficacy: The exercise of control*. New York, NY: Freeman.

Betts, M.J., Forbes S.L., & L.A. Livingston. (2007). Factors contributing to the attrition of Canadian amateur ice hockey officials: The experiences of referees and linesmen in Atlantic Canada. *Avante, 11*, 15.

Catteeuw, P., Helsen, W., Gilis, B., & Wagemans, J. (2009). Decision-making skills, role specificity, and deliberate practice in association football refereeing. *Journal of Sports Sciences, 27*(11), 1125–1136, doi:10.1080/02640410903079179

Colley, R.C., Garriguet, D., Janssen, I., Craig, C. L., Clarke, J., & Tremblay, M.S. (2011). Physical activity of Canadian children and youth: Accelerometer results from the 2007 to 2009 Canadian Health Measures Survey. *Health Reports, 22*(1), 15–23.

Cook, S.L., & Sladowski, P.S. (2013). *Volunteering and older adults: Final Report* (ISBN: 978-1-926530-14-7). Retrieved from Volunteer Canada, Human Resources and Skill Development Canada, Community Development and Partnership Directorate website:__https://volunteer.ca/vdemo/Engaging Volunteers_DOCS/Volunteering_and_Older_Adults_Final_Report_2013.pdf

Côté, J., Baker, J., & Abernethy, B. (2007). Practice and play in the development of sport expertise. *Handbook of Sport Psychology, 3*, 184–202.

Côté, J., & Fraser-Thomas, J. (2016). Youth involvement and positive development in sport. In P.R.E. Crocker (Ed.), *Sport and exercise psychology: A Canadian perspective* (pp. 256–287). Toronto: Pearson.

Cuskelly, G., Evans, G., & Hoye, R. (2004). Problems and issues in the recruitment and retention of sports officials: A report prepared for the Australian Sports Commission. Griffith University, Griffith Business School, Brisbane, Australia.

Cuskelly, G., & Hoye, R. (2013). Sports officials' intention to continue. *Sport Management Review, 16*(4), 451–464. doi:10.1016/j.smr.2013.01.003

Davids, K., Güllich, A., Shuttleworth, R., & Araújo, D. (2017). Understanding environmental and task constraints on talent development: Analysis of microstructure of practice and macro-structure of developmental histories. In J. Baker, S. Cobley, J. Schorer, & N. Wattie (Eds.), *The Routledge handbook of talent identification and development* (pp. 80–98). New York: Routledge.

Deci, E. L., & Ryan, R. M. (1985). The general causality orientations scale: Self-determination in personality. *Journal of Research in Personality, 19*(2), 109–134.

Ericsson, K. A., & Harwell, K. W. (2019). Deliberate practice and proposed limits on the effects of practice on the acquisition of expert performance: Why the original definition maters and recommendations for future research. *Frontiers in Psychology, 10,* 2396. doi:10.3389/fpsyg.2019.02396

Ericsson, K. A., Krampe, R. T., & Tesch-Romer, C. (1993). The role of deliberate practice in the acquisition of expert performance. *Psychological Review, 100,* 363–406.

Farrow, D., Reid, M., Buszard, T., & Kovalchik, S. (2018). Charting the development of sport expertise: Challenges and opportunities. *International Review of Sport and Exercise Psychology, 11,* 238–257.

Forbes, S.L., & Livingston, L.A. (2013). Changing the call: Rethinking attrition and retention in the ice hockey officiating ranks. *Sport in Society, 16,* 295–309.

Forbes, S.L., Livingston, L.A., & Thevakumar, D. (2018). *Sport officiating in Canada: An overview and analysis of organizational resources and supports.* Unpublished report.Ford, P., De Ste Croix, M., Lloyd, R., Meyers, R., Moosavi, M., Oliver, J., Till, K., & Williams, C. (2011). The long-term athlete development model: Physiological evidence and application. *Journal of Sports Sciences, 29,* 389–402.

Fowler, B., Smith, J., Nordstrom, H., & Ferguson, T. (2019). Ice hockey officiating retention: A qualitative understanding of junior ice hockey officials' motivations in Canada, *Managing Sport and Leisure, 24,* 18–31, doi:10.1080/23750472.2019.1565944

Gagné, F. (2004). Transforming gifts into talents: The DMGT as a developmental theory. *High Ability Studies, 15,* 119–147.

Gladwell, M. (2008). *Outliers: The story of success.* Boston, MA: Little, Brown and Company.

Gulbin, J.P., Croser, M.J., Morley, E.J., & Weissensteiner, J.R. (2013). An integrated framework for the optimisation of sport and athlete development: A practitioner approach. *Journal of Sports Sciences, 31,* 1319–1331.

Güllich, A. (2019). "Macro-structure" of developmental participation histories and "micro-structure" of practice of German female world-class and national-class football players. *Journal of Sports Sciences, 37,* 1347–1355.

Hambrick, D.Z., Burgoyne, A.P., Macnamara, B.N., & Ullén, F. (2018). Toward a multifactorial model of expertise: Beyond born versus made. *Annals of the New York Academy of Sciences.* doi:10.1111/nyas.13586

Hambrick, D.Z., Oswald, F.L., Altmann, E.M., Meinz, E.J., Gobet, F., & Campitelli, G. (2014). Deliberate practice: Is that all it takes to become an expert? *Intelligence, 45,* 34–56.

Hancock, D.J., Dawson, D.J., & Auger, D. (2015). Why Ref? Understanding sport officials' motivations to begin, continue, and quit. *Movement & Sport Sciences-Science & Motricité, 87,* 31–39.

Hong, E., Jeong, Y., & Downward, P. (2019). Perceived organizational support, internal motivation, and work-family conflict among soccer referees. *Managing Sport and Leisure, 24,* 141–154. doi:10.1080/23750472.2019.1593049.

Kellett, P., & Shilbury, D. (2007). Umpire participation: Is abuse really the issue? *Sport Management Review, 10*(3), 209–229. doi:10.1016/S1441–3523 (07)70012-8

Koz, D., Fraser-Thomas, J., & Baker, J. (2012). Accuracy of professional sports drafts in predicting career potential. *Scandinavian Journal of Medicine and Science in Sports, 22*, e64–e69. doi:10.1111/j.1600–0838.2011.01408.x

Livingston, L. A., & Forbes, S. L. (2007). Factors contributing to the attrition of Canadian amateur ice hockey officials: Survey results from an Ontario-based district hockey association. *Avante, 11*(1), 1–14.

Livingston, L.A., & Forbes, S.L. (2016). Factors contributing to the retention of Canadian amateur sport officials: Motivations, perceived organizational support, and resilience. *International Journal of Sports Science & Coaching, 11*(3), 342–355.

Mack, D.E., Sabiston, C.M., McDonough, M.H., Wilson, P.M., & Paskevich, D.M. (2016). Motivation and behavior change. In P.R.E. Crocker (Ed.), *Sport and Exercise Psychology: A Canadian Perspective* (pp. 52–82). Toronto: Pearson.

Mack, M., Schulenkorf, N., Adair, D., & Bennie, A. (2018). Factors influencing the development of elite-level sports officials in Australia: The AFL, ABA and FFA. *Sport in Society, 21*(9), 1240–1257. doi:10.1080/17430437.2017. 1388781

MacMahon, C., Helsen, W. F., Starkes, J. L., & Weston, M. (2007). Decision-making skills and deliberate practice in elite association football referees. *Journal of Sports Sciences, 25*(1), 65–78.

MacMahon, C., Mascarenhas, D., Plessner, H., Pizzera, A., Oudejans, R., & Raab, M. (2015). London: Routledge.

MacMahon, C., & Rix-Liévre, G. (2019, July). Modelling and supporting the career development of sport officials. In Presentation at the *European federation of sport and exercise psychology congress.* University of Münster, Germany.

Macnamara, B.N., Hambrick, D.Z., & Oswald, F.L. (2014). Deliberate practice and performance in music, games, sports, education, and professions: A meta-analysis. *Psychological Science, 25*, 1608–1618.

Maher, J.P., Doerksen, S.E., Elavsky, S., Hyde, A.L., Pincus, A.L., Ram, N., & Conroy, D.E. (2013). A daily analysis of physical activity and satisfaction with life in emerging adults. *Health Psychology, 32*(6), 647–656.

Mascarenhas, D. R. D., Collins, D., & Mortimer, P. (2005). Elite refereeing performance: Developing a model for sport science support. *The Sport Psychologist, 19*, 364–379.

Misener, K., & Doherty, A. (2009). A case study of organizational capacity in nonprofit community sport. *Journal of Sport Management, 23*(4), 457–482.

Myers, N.D., Feltz, D.L., Guillén, F., & Dithurbide, L. (2012). Development of, and initial validity evidence for, the reference self-efficacy scale: A multistudy report. *Journal of Sport & Exercise Psychology, 34*, 737–765.

Nichols, G., & James, M. (2008). One size does not fit all: Implications of sports club diversity for their effectiveness as a policy tool and for government support. *Managing Leisure, 13*(2), 104–114.

Ollis, S., Macpherson, A., & Collins, D. (2006). Expertise and talent development in rugby refereeing: An ethnographic enquiry. *Journal of Sports Sciences, 24,* 309–322.

Pina, J.A., Passos, A., Araújo, D., & Maynard, M.T. (2018). Football refereeing: An integrative review. *Psychology of Sport & Exercise, 35,* 10–26.

Robinson, K., Wattie, N., Schorer, J., & Baker, J. (2018). Talent identification in sport: A systematic review of 25 years of research. *Sports Medicine, 48,* 97–109.

Sabaini, D. (2001). *How to get and keep officials.* A special report published by the National Association of Sport Officials (NASO).

Sam, M. P., Andrew, J. C., & Gee, S. (2018). The modernisation of umpire development: Netball New Zealand's reforms and impacts. *European Sport Management Quarterly, 18*(3), 263–286.

Simonton, D.K. (2017). Does talent exist? Yes! In J. Baker, S. Cobley, J. Schorer, & N. Wattie (Eds.), *The Routledge handbook of talent identification and development in sport* (pp. 11–18). London: Routledge.

Syed, M. (2010). *Bounce: Mozart, Federer, Picasso, Beckham and the science of success.* New York, NY: Harper.

Titlebaum, P. J., Haberlin, N., & Titlebaum, G. (2009). Recruitment and retention of sports officials. *Recreational Sports Journal, 33*(2), 102–108.

Warner, S., Tingle, J. K., & Kellett, P. (2013). Officiating attrition: The experiences of former referees via a sport development lens. *Journal of Sport Management, 27*(4), 316–328.

8 Evaluating Your Officiating Development Program

Program evaluation involves systematically collecting, tracking, and analyzing information (data) about some undertaking your organization is engaged in. Evaluation is important because it helps your organization understand if what they are doing is an effective and efficacious approach. For example, your organization developed and implemented a new way of training your officials that takes into account their particular sport and participation demands, and now you want to see if the training program did what you intended and/or if the way you chose to conduct it is going as planned. There can be myths about what program evaluation is (e.g., the purpose is to only prove existing program success or failure) and requires (e.g., the need for outside expert evaluators) (Patton, 2008). While these can certainly be elements of program evaluation, centrally, what evaluation should focus on is utility, relevance, and practicality to the context in question. In addition, evaluation should be carried out through a reflexive and reflective process aimed to transfer gathered *knowledge to action* (Graham et al., 2006), which is what many high-profile health organizations advocate (WHO, 2019). Similar lessons can be applied to officiating development programming, structures, and evaluation.

Clearly defining the components of your development program is critical to an effective evaluation. Knowing what's involved with each of those components, how they were delivered, and what they are meant to achieve underpins that understanding. In other words, a systematic and representative evaluation helps you understand your organizational activities better, see the impact they have, and plan for future activity (Patton, 2008).

This chapter outlines a practical, step-wise cyclical framework to help organize and arrange your program evaluation activities and to lay stake to the importance of such activities' use and timing along the evaluation process. But, first, establishing a clearer understanding about different types of program evaluation is a useful starting point for choosing an evaluation strategy that best serves your officiating level, short- or long-term organizational mission, and organizational capacity.

Types of Program Evaluations

Just as there are different things to evaluate, there are different approaches to carrying out such evaluation. An important first step is to know what you want to evaluate about your officiating development program and why: Then you can identify the best approach. Table 8.1 provides some examples of different evaluation types, when they might be best used, the potential results you can expect from their implementation, and what makes each type crucial to the evaluation process.

While it's important to know that there can be different options/approaches to evaluating programs, it is equally important to remember – one size does not fit all.

A Practical Approach to Program Evaluation

The following diagram lays out the steps to guide you in conducting your evaluation (Figure 8.1). Each step provides an indication of what

Table 8.1 Types of program evaluation

Type of Evaluation	When to Use	Expected Results	Why Is It Important?
Formative	• Development/ planning process • Modifying an existing program	• Identify needed resources • Target audience • Feasibility	• Resource planning • Modifications required • Assess potential success
Process	• Starts with program implementation • Runs through life of program	• What's working or not working • If implemented as planned • Meeting needs of, or reaches target audience	• Early warning about problems • Ongoing monitoring
Outcome	• After program is underway	• Program impact • Achieving (or not) program goals	• Shows effectiveness of program
Impact	• After program is underway • At different points in time • At the end of the program	• How well the program met the desired goals	• Degree of success of the program • Future planning

Adapted from Centers for Disease and Prevention Control (CDC, 2011).

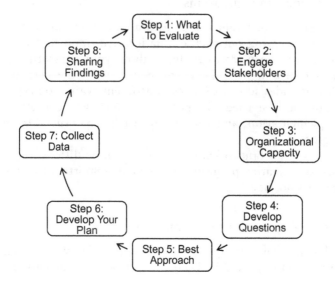

Figure 8.1 Steps in the evaluation cycle.

should be done and why it's important. We also provide you with some tips on how to approach each of them. You'll notice that this is circular in nature. That's because ensuring quality programs requires ongoing evaluation.

Step 1: Knowing What to Evaluate

A clearly defined evaluation (e.g., specific target, activities, goals, etc.) helps your organization remain focused and also assists in determining whether doing an evaluation is feasible given the information/resources available. An important consideration in evaluating effects of your sport official development programming on officials' themselves should be to recognize the range of malleable (changeable and more adaptive over time) and stable factors (more fixed over time) (see Chapter 4) that can be tracked and compared. For example, individual factors such as perceived organizational support, motivation, and self-efficacy are quantifiable and easily gathered through questionnaires or survey approaches.

Additionally, other sport participants who interact with officials (e.g., coaches, players, administrators) may be a valuable resource for evaluative information depending on what components you are assessing. For example, coaches and athletes may be able to speak to how the officiating development program impacted their participation in the sport. It's also useful to explore other factors that may affect the comprehensiveness of your evaluation. For example, if your program includes a post-match debrief for novice officials, or examines their individual tasks within a given environment, as well as their interactions with other officials, this can shed light on how well your program is preparing them to officiate. Knowing what factors, processes, and outcomes to evaluate within the climate of your officiating development program requires careful consideration at this stage in the activity of program assessment.

Logic *models* offer a practical guide for mapping and identifying what you are evaluating. *Logic models* visually describe the relationship between resources used, activities undertaken to implement/coordinate the program, and what your organization intends to achieve with the program. Table 8.2 presents an example of what this might look like.

How to know what to evaluate:

- Start by building your logic model.

  - Start with a clear description of what you are going to evaluate (e.g., development program).
  - Include all the goals, activities, and outcomes of the program under consideration

- Determine the purpose of the evaluation (see Table 8.1).
- Identify the primary users/beneficiaries of the evaluation (i.e., other primary stakeholders).

Table 8.2 Sample logic model

Program: [Insert title and/or brief description]
Goal: [Briefly identify the main/primary goal of the program]

Inputs	Activities	Outcomes		
		• Outcomes reflect what was accomplished by/through the activities undertaken		
		Short Term	Intermediate	Long Term
• Inputs are what your organization invested in the program • Examples include staff, training materials, time, etc.	• Activities reflect what your organization did related to the program • Examples include delivering information sessions, training sessions, communication bulletins, etc.	• These reflect immediate effects	• Intermediate outcomes are achieved over time	• These are achieved closer to the end of the program or over a longer period of time

Tips:

1   Ask, who should be included in the evaluation?
2   Consider the resources you have available to bring people onboard (e.g., online meetings, communication strategies).
3   Consider pre- and during-season/competition timing when stakeholders are mutually present with one another (e.g., tournaments, pre-season preparation conferencing).

Step 2: Engaging Stakeholders

Key types of stakeholders (e.g., those with a vested interest in the program) can include, in addition to your officials, your sport's executives and managerial personnel, other officiating managers within and outside the organization, and those directly or indirectly impacted by sport officials' participation (officiating trainers and coaches, athletic or team coaches, athletes/players, and even spectatorship). Building support and 'buy-in' for an evaluation from stakeholders can help increase their awareness of the evaluation process. Engaging stakeholders can have the long-term benefit of support for any recommendations coming out of the evaluation. Stakeholder involvement also helps increase objectivity and improve communication about the evaluation. Stakeholders also provide another "set of eyes" to help ensure you haven't missed any important details (CDC, 1999). Additionally, engaging stakeholders lets you build trust in the program and the organization's work, demonstrates accountability, and gives a voice to those with little or no voice in the organizational operations. When engaging stakeholders, it is important to consider a multidimensional approach. Certainly, stakeholders closest to the activity, such as officials, coaches, players, parents, and administrators, will be essential to engage. But it may also be useful to engage more distant stakeholders, such as industry professionals (e.g., Human Resources), other sports personnel (e.g., officiating coordinators from another sport), and academics (researchers and graduate students). For example, researchers whose area of expertise and interest relates to officiating sport science, or more generally to sport science or human resource management, can be valuable partners in evaluating programs. They can collaborate to inform *what* to evaluate and *how* (see Steps 4 and 5). Partnering with researchers can also provide a way to extending the organizational capacity to evaluation programs (see Step 3). Researchers and/or graduate students can help to collect and manage data (sometime even being embedded with an organization), thereby facilitating program evolution without extra burden to proximal stakeholders. After knowing what to evaluate, a next process needs to be building confidence, visibility, and acceptance for recommendations that will eventually divulge from the program evaluation.

How to engage stakeholders:

- Identify all your stakeholders:

  - Stakeholders are individuals/groups who have an interest in the program, may be impacted by the program, and could be affected by the evaluation (e.g., program participants, staff responsible for implementation, decision-makers, organization board).

- Understand stakeholders' roles, interests, expectations of the program, and evaluation:

  - Some stakeholder roles will be clear; others may require some additional information and/or analysis. Consider the purpose, preoccupations, and interaction between various stakeholder roles.

- Determine the best way to get them involved (e.g., formal or informal meetings, traveling "road show", online meeting, and knowledge dissemination forums to accommodate stakeholder time, engagement, and interest levels).

Tips:

- Ask, who should be included in the evaluation?
- Consider the resources you have available to bring people onboard (e.g., online meetings, communication strategies).
- Consider pre- and during-season/competition timing when stakeholders are mutually present with one another (e.g., tournaments, pre-season preparation conferencing).

Step 3: Determining Your Organizational Capacity

Steps 1 and 2 ask you to consider what you want to do and who needs to be involved. Step 3 helps you understand what you're capable of doing with respect to the evaluation. As noted above, no two organizations are the same and each organization has to be aware of what it's capable of doing. Evaluations are resource-intensive (e.g., time, in-kind support), even if you can hire an external consultant. Knowing what your organization can do is dictated by its capacity, which consists of human resources (e.g., human capital, enthusiasm, skills, knowledge), financial resources (e.g., revenues, expenses), infrastructure (e.g., formalized organization, communication strategies, facilities), planning and development (e.g., strategic plan, implementation processes and supports), and external relations (e.g., community partners, bureaucratic partnerships: Doherty, Misener, & Cuskelly, 2014). Understanding capacity is necessary to clearly establish the difference between what you would *like* to evaluate and what you *can* evaluate. Ultimately, depending on capacity, it will probably be necessary to prioritize what is evaluated.

How to determine your organization's capacity:

- Revisit what you want to evaluate.

  - Be clear about what you want to look at and why.
  - Use this to focus on identifying resources.

- Identify the resources you'll need to carry out the evaluation.

  - Think ideal scenario and explore all the potential resources you might need.

- Examine your internal personnel.

  - Leverage your internal resources to help carry out the work.

- Examine external partnerships.

  - There may be people outside your organization willing to help (e.g., local universities).
  - Consider your existing networks; you may be able to access "experts" from a wider area.

- Consider the financial resources you may need.

  - In-kind contributions (e.g., volunteer pro-bono assistance)
  - Assess whether you can carry out the evaluation without having to hire someone.

- Assess the timing of the evaluation.

Tips:

- You may have people on staff/volunteers who have experience with evaluation.
- There may be people who have experience doing research.
- There may be people outside your organization willing to help (e.g., local universities).
- Consider your existing networks; you may be able to access "experts" from a wider area.

Step 4: Developing Your Evaluation Questions

Developing your questions helps you frame your evaluation (e.g., what will be asked, who will be asked, etc.). There are two categories of questions useful for program evaluation. The first is *Key Evaluation Questions* (KEQs), which are informed by the type of evaluation you are conducting (e.g., process, outcome, cost-benefit). KEQs are meant to address higher-level questions about the program and relate to the overall performance of the program (e.g., whether it worked, was implemented accordingly, was worth the investment). KEQs can also be helpful in framing your evaluation report. Table 8.3 provides examples of evaluation questions based on categories that you can use in your evaluation.

The second type of questions relates to whether the program was appropriate, effective, and efficient. These types of questions allow you to dig deeper into whether the program achieved what you intended in the best way possible (see Table 8.4). Keep in mind, the questions you ask depend on the type of evaluation you are conducting (e.g., process, outcome, cost-benefit).

Thinking about your evaluation questions using these suggestions will allow you to review your program in a detailed manner.

Table 8.3 Key evaluation questions (KEQs)

Evaluation Type	Example Questions
Process evaluation	How was the program implemented? Did the program reach its target audience? Was the program availability well advertised?
Outcome evaluation	Did the program work as intended? Did the program achieve the intended outcomes/goals? Did anything unexpected come up? Did other factors influence the success of the program?
Cost-benefit evaluation	Did the program use resources effectively? Did the benefits of the program outweigh the costs? Was this program the most cost-effective way to address the issue?

Table 8.4 Sample evaluation questions by evaluation focus

Evaluation Type	Example Questions
Program fit	How well did the program fit with the organization's priorities? Was the program the best fit for addressing the organization's need(s)?
Program effectiveness	Did the program work produce worthwhile outcomes? Did the program achieve the proposed results in the time identified?
Program value	Did the program provide a positive return on investment? Did the inputs and outputs related to the program support the desired outcomes?

For additional resources, visit https://www.betterevaluation.org/en/rainbow_framework/frame/specify_key_evaluation_questions)

How to develop your evaluation questions:

- Revisit your program description through the lens of the above categories and determine the program status (e.g., stage of development).
- Determine what "success" means for the program under evaluation.
  - Select key stakeholders who can assist with this stage.
  - Work with those key stakeholders to identify the criteria to be used for determining success.
  - These will be used as benchmarks for assessing the answers to your DOQs.
- Ask the different stakeholder groups for evaluation questions.
- Compare questions to the program description and stage of development.
  - Consider combining strongly similar questions.
  - Eliminate duplicate questions and those not relevant to the stage of development (e.g., outcome questions not relevant for planning evaluation).
- Be open to any/all questions but be prepared to refine them for data collection purposes.
- Share questions with stakeholders to develop an acceptable list.

Tips:

- Provide stakeholders with the program description and remind them of the evaluation purpose(s); this will help them frame their questions.
- Engaging stakeholders throughout this step will help ensure relevant areas are explored.
- Process-focused questions explore if the program was implemented as planned and is reaching its target audience. Outcome-focused questions determine how successful the program is in achieving its goals/objectives.
- Solid questions will influence what data you collect and how, how that data will be analyzed, and how best to report it.

Step 5: Identifying the Best Way to Collect Data

How you collect data (e.g., qualitative, quantitative, mixed methods) depends on what you are assessing and available resources. Data collection influences your ability to effectively answer your evaluation questions. In the end, your data should be credible and appropriate to the questions you've asked. Those same questions should inform which method or methods you choose. Collecting data can be facilitated by a variety of software tools for analyzing qualitative and quantitative data. Many offer free trials for a short period of time, while others are free as "open-source" tools. Most also offer online training tutorials. What, if anything you choose to use, should be dictated by your organizational resources (human and financial), the nature of the evaluation, and the time available to carry out the work. Here, we present a table of different data collection strategies you can choose from.

How to identify the best way to collect your data:

- Revisit the purpose of the evaluation and your evaluation questions.
- Develop your data collection strategy.
  - Identify what you will measure (e.g., what data do you need to answer your evaluation questions).
  - Determine the program stage for collecting data (e.g., start, middle, end), as well as your data collecting timeline (e.g., start state, finish date for evaluation).
  - Choose your data collection method (quantitative, qualitative, both).
  - Identify who will be asked to respond to the questions.
  - Determine how you will ask your evaluation questions (e.g., questionnaires, document reviews, analysis of existing data, one-on-one and/or focus group interviews).
- Consider ethical issues (confidentiality, anonymity, securing the data).
- Determine the best format for your questions (e.g., ranking, scales, dropdown list, open ended, etc.).

Tips (*questions worth asking*):

- What do we need to know about the program to make informed decisions?
- What are the different ways we can realistically collect data?
- Who is going to do the data collection?
  - Do we have the skills/abilities to use these different methods?
  - If no, do we need help and/or training?
- Can this information be collected in a timely, practical, and cost-efficient manner?
- Can you use pre-existing surveys?
- How can this information be analyzed once it's collected?

Step 6: Develop Your Evaluation Plan

A well thought out plan (e.g., how you'll do the work) is your roadmap to conducting a comprehensive, focused, and timely evaluation. Your evaluation plan also serves as a framework for your evaluation report (discussed below). The following outlines key elements of your evaluation plan.

Key elements of an evaluation plan

1   Introduction
    This section includes a concise description of the program (e.g., focus) being evaluated, why the evaluation is being carried out (i.e., purpose), and what your major evaluation questions are. The program logic model can provide some information for this section, but it is also helpful to consider what you might expect from the evaluation (e.g., what you hope to learn, decisions arising from the evaluation).

2   Audience
    Audience refers to the group who you will share the evaluation results with. Knowing who your audience is influences what data are collected and how that information is presented to them. For example, if you are sharing the results with your officials, you may choose to look at data related to effective program delivery. On the other hand, if you are presenting to the Board of Governors, they may be more interested in the cost-effectiveness of the program.

3   Relevant questions
    Reflect on your key and related evaluation questions. These inform your evaluation and include sources of information, data collection methods, and your analysis. It is helpful to present your KEQs in this section to help frame the subsequent elements.

4   Information and Resources
    Use this section to identify what you will need to conduct the evaluation. For example, what information do you need to answer your evaluation questions and where can you get that information? Identifying relevant information also requires consideration of number of participants (e.g., how many people do you want to complete a questionnaire or participate in a focus group). Resources considerations include, but are not limited to, human (e.g., staff to data collection; research collaborators to assist with data analysis), data collection instruments (e.g., online questionnaires), financial (e.g., budget to carry out data collection), and equipment (e.g., computers for data analysis).

5   Data collection strategies
    This element focuses on "how" you will collect your information (data). Using several different techniques (see Table 8.5) increases your depth of understanding, as well as the quality of your results. Your strategies should also identify who will carry out the data collection, as well as a timeline for information gathering.

6   Data analysis
    Data analysis involves identifying techniques for making sense of the information (data) you will collect. Your analysis is informed by the type of information you collect. For example, if you conduct

interviews your data are in the form of text. These can be analyzed using basic techniques such as key word searches of the answers given. Or, if you have the organizational capacity, you can use software (e.g., open source or purchased) to perform the analysis. If you use questionnaires and collect numerical data, you could conduct various statistical analyses (e.g., frequency distributions, descriptive analysis). As with qualitative data, software is also available for this type of analysis. Or, if you have the budget, you could engage an experienced research to perform the relevant analyses.

Table 8.5 Types of data collection methods

Method	Why Use	Strengths	Drawbacks	Resource Requirement
Questionnaires	When you need information from many people in a short period of time	• Inexpensive (e.g., free online services) • Easy to administer (e.g., online) • Analysis is fairly easy • Anonymous responses	• May not get sufficient detail • Impersonal • Creating good questions may be difficult	Low
One-on-One interviews	When you want to get more in-depth information	• Helps build relationships with stakeholders • Degree of flexibility • Detailed information	• Time consuming • Analysis is more difficult • May be costly • Interviewers need to be skilled	Medium-High
Secondary analysis	When you have existing information available (e.g., feedback forms, exit surveys)	• Don't need to create new instrument • Information already exists • Can be done without seeking participants	• Can be time consuming • Information may be incomplete • Limited to what already exists	Moderate
Focus groups	When you want more information from several people	• Less time consuming that interviews • Get general perceptions quickly • Provides depth of information	• Analysis can be difficult • Requires a good facilitator • Scheduling numerous people is difficult	Medium-High

7   Information sharing
    While this element is fleshed out fully in the final evaluation report, including a brief description of the proposed method. This is an opportunity to identify who will complete the report (e.g., internal staff versus a hired consultant), as well as what the final report will look like (e.g., written report, public presentation). Finally, consideration should be given to whether you need different versions of report if you have more than one audience (Evaluation plan components adapted from Jason (2008) and Owen & Rogers (2001)).

How to develop an evaluation plan:

- Start by writing down the purpose of the evaluation. A purpose defines the intentions and destination for your evaluation plan.
- Detail the data collection strategy by identifying the following:
    - Stage of the evaluation (e.g., beginning, end).
    - Start and end date for the evaluation.
    - Data collection method(s) to be used (i.e., quantitative, qualitative, both).
    - The evaluation participants (e.g., officials, board members, staff).
    - Data collection tools to be used (e.g., questionnaires, focus groups).
    - Ethical issues and how they will be managed.
- Assign responsibilities (e.g., who is doing what).
- Indicate how the results of the evaluation will be used/shared.
- Write your plan out carefully with as much detail as possible.

Tips:

- Get feedback from key stakeholders to ensure evaluation plan makes sense.
- Be specific when identifying evaluation activities, responsibilities, deadlines, resources.
- Consider using a data collection matrix to help identify potential sources of information (see example below).

Step 7: Collect Your Data/Information

Gathering credible data/information to answer each evaluation question effectively is an important step leading to useful results and for making viable recommendations. Data collection starts by choosing the data collection methods that align with your organization's resources and capacity (revisit Table 8.1). Once the data are collected, it is important to sort and categorize them based on predefined characteristics (e.g., by respondent type, based on question answered, etc.). Data organization is driven by purpose and goals of the evaluation. For example, if you are interested in your officials' perception of perceived organizational support, include the question in your evaluation, then categorize their responses by officiating level, years of experience, and/or gender. What kind of data do you want to examine? What other factors are worth considering? (e.g., gender, geography, age). Can these be paired with individual characteristics such as self-efficacy, commitment to learnings, satisfaction, or skill improvement?

How to collect your data/information:

- Develop your data collection tools (e.g., questionnaires, interview questions).
- Identify the data collection activities (e.g., how you will actually collect data).
  - If using web-based data collection services, set up questionnaire/survey online.
- Train those individuals who will be collecting the data.
- Establish data collection schedule.

Tips:

- Check within your organization to see if anyone has experience with data collection.
- Consider collaborating with an area university as they'll have folks with this skillset.
  - They might even have students needing work-related placements.
- Keep the data collection simply if you're new to doing this.
- Let time and human resources guide your choices.

Step 8: Report and Support Use of Findings

Findings are only useful if they are shared with those who may directly benefit from them. This is one reason we undertake program evaluation and assessment, in order to evaluate our own organizational activities in ways that help influence future decision-making but help others interpret our plans and organizational choices we've implemented. Effectively communicating the data and findings we've generated helps to prove and disprove our approaches, but similarly, provides a vehicle for others affected to view the issues. Also, findings need to be translated into terminology relevant to different stakeholders and synthesized to effectively communicate the key messages provided by the findings. The design of recommendations should illuminate your findings in ways that use the data to position new development approaches or adaptions that are needed. Your final report, regardless of form, should consider the following questions:

- Who needs to respond to and make decisions based on your findings?
- Have you included everyone who may be interested in your evaluation as part of your audience?
- Have you presented your finding in a way that allows your audience to understand the results in a meaningful way?
- Have you presented the information in the most effective way based on your audience?
- How much time will each audience want to spend looking at your findings?
- Have you overlooked anything? (Adapted from https://www.ahrq. gov/talkingquality/assess/evaluation-plan.html).

How to report and support the use of your findings:

- Determine your reporting requirements (e.g., due date, format).
- Tailor reporting format to intended users (e.g., club administration, board, etc.).
  - Format type can take many forms (e.g., executive summaries, presentations, written/oral reports, bulletins, etc.).
- Present findings in a way that is usable by intended audience.
- Develop recommendations.
- Develop a communication strategy to share the information both initially and long term.

Tips:

- Write and present your findings in a way that is clear to and understandable by the lay person (e.g., plain language).
- Consider following the 1:3:25 principle:
  - One (1) page highlighting the key/main points of the evaluation, including recommendations.
  - Three (3) pages that concisely summarize findings for those who don't have time to read the full report.
  - Twenty-five pages (+/–) that provide background on the evaluation (issue, why evaluation needed), description of how the evaluation was carried out, evaluation questions explored, and the findings and conclusions.
- Recommendations identify not only what can/needs to be adjusted, but also how those changes can be accomplished.

Summary

Simply put, evaluation of any program is important. Intuitively you may recognize the value of your program, but you have to demonstrate that to others (e.g., key decision-makers, those who have budget control). In other words, you have to show whether the program worked and that's only possible with data. There are also other benefits to evaluation. For example, evaluation demonstrates that resources were allocated appropriately.

An evaluation also lets you explain to others what happened. This is fleshed out in the logic model to a certain degree, but it also becomes evident by asking key questions – what happened? What worked? What didn't work? What can be improved on? A carefully planned evaluation also lets you focus on understanding how the program met its anticipated goals. This information can then be used to make improvements. Evaluation may also reveal unanticipated outcomes (e.g., delivering on-line learning to communities with limited internet access), which can also lead to program improvements.

Carefully planned evaluations also give a voice to those who may not usually have one (e.g., including the voice of an entry-level official). Also, those voices vary according to the role an individual occupies. For example, a board member has a different role and different perspective from an officiating coordinator. Allowing diverse voices to be heard provides a more complete picture of a program's impact.

This chapter has outlined the typical approaches to and components of program evaluation. But it is important to remember that each organization is different, even within the same sport. In other words, one size does not fit all! Understanding organization capacity, including resources you may have at hand (e.g., community partners who are experienced in evaluation or students who have taken research methods courses), can help you develop and carry out your evaluation. Capacity can make a big difference in developing an effective evaluation.

TAKE AWAY MESSAGES FROM THIS CHAPTER

- *Know what you're evaluating*: Clearly define evaluation targets, activities, and goals to help your organization remain focused.
- *Engage your stakeholders*: Build 'buy-in' for your evaluation through increasing stakeholders' awareness of the process and foster confidence in evaluation recommendations.
- *Plan your evaluation carefully*: Detail the purpose of your evaluation and pick an appropriate data collection strategy.

(Continued)

- *Get the best data you can*: Gather and track your data carefully and use methods that fit your capacity (i.e., questionnaires, focus groups).
- *Share the evaluation results in a meaningful way*: Consider ways you make your findings apparent and transparent to others impacted by your officiating development program (i.e., officials, other sport participants, sport managers).
- *Follow through on the recommendations:* Take practical steps to transfer knowledge gained into impactful and pragmatic actions and organizational activities (Graham et al., 2006).

References

Centers for Disease Control and Prevention. (1999). Framework for program evaluation in public health. *MMWR Recommendations and Reports, 48*(RR-11). Retrieved December 31, 2018, from http://www.cdc.gov/mmwr/preview/mmwrhtml/rr4811a1.htm

Centers for Disease Control and Prevention. (2011). Developing an effective evaluation plan. Retrieved December 22, 2018, from https://www.cdc.gov/obesity/downloads/CDC-Evaluation-Workbook-508.pdf

Doherty, A., Misener, K., & Cuskelly, G. (2014). Toward a multidimensional framework of capacity in community sport clubs. *Nonprofit and Voluntary Sector Quarterly, 43*(2_suppl), 124S–142S.

Graham, I.D., Logan, J., Harrison, M.B., Straus, S.E., Tetroe, J., Caswell, W., & Robinson, N. (2006). Lost in knowledge translation: Time for a map? *Journal of Continuing Education in the Health Professions, 26*(1), 13–24.

Jason, M.H. (2008). *Evaluating programs to increase student achievement.* Thousand Oaks, CA: SAGE Publications, Inc. doi: 10.4135/9781412990264

Owen, J., & Rogers, P. (2001). *Program evaluation.* London: SAGE Publications Ltd.

Patton, M.Q. (2008). *Utilization-focused evaluation* (4th ed.). Thousand Oaks, CA: Sage Publications.

World Health Organization. (2019). *Knowledge-to-Action Framework (KTA).* Retrieved from https://www.who.int/reproductivehealth/topics/best_practices/greatproject_KTAframework/en/

Other Resource

For more information and resources on program evaluation visit: https://www.betterevaluation.org/en

9   Emerging Issues in Sport and Sport Officiating

We wrote this book because we, and a growing number of sport science researchers around the world, see officials as an indispensable part of organized sport. They bring structure and fairness to competitions by upholding the spirit and letter of the law in an effort to provide all participants with opportunities to compete and perform in environments that are safe, fair, and equitable. The overwhelming majority of officials, moreover, are well intentioned and show selfless concern for the wellbeing of others when plying their trade. They *want* to do their best and they *try* to do their best because they understand that their performance and actions have the potential to influence the outcome of the contest. They also know that competitive sport environments may yield dissent from players, coaches, team officials, and spectators, and that such opposition intends to challenge both their decisions (i.e., the call) and their choices in how to respond (i.e., the penalty that is imposed). From a historical perspective, rightly or wrongly, sport officials have long coped with those who question their authority and competence. These challenges remain today. However, in a world of sport filled with growing expectations underpinned by commercial interests and technological change, real or perceived errors in judgment risk encountering immediate criticism and blame on a global scale.

It is time to admit that the culture of sport has changed considerably over the last half century and that it will continue to change going forward. With continued shifts to the sporting landscape, there will inevitably be far-reaching effects on the ways sport officials participate and perform. Therefore, the purpose of this chapter is to explore some important and emerging issues in the realm of sport and their implications for the future recruitment, training, development, and advancement of the next generation of sport officials. While there are certainly multiple themes that deserve attention going forward, we have limited our discussion to what we see as three critical topics: The professionalization of youth sport; technology and officiating decision-making; and equity, diversity, and inclusion. Unless adequately addressed, these emerging themes have the potential to continue to undermine efforts to recruit, develop, retain, and advance sport officials that have been discussed in detail within this book.

The Professionalization of Youth Sport

The professionalization of youth sport was first brought to light some 40 years ago when Jonathon Brower, an associate professor of sociology at California State University – Fullerton, wrote about the growing seriousness and importance ascribed to youth sport (Brower, 1979). Using Little League Baseball as an example, Brower explored how youth sport was effectively imitating its professional counterpart while at the same time highlighting the dominance of the win ethic, the privileging of the best athletes, overbearing parents and coaches, and the legitimization of hostility toward the umpire. While not a new phenomenon, the professionalization of youth sport has arguably expanded over time beyond mainstream male-dominated professional sports (e.g., baseball, football, ice hockey, basketball, and soccer) to include all sports whereby a youth athlete of any sex or gender orientation has an opportunity to compete at an elite level (e.g., college or university athletics, Olympic Games). Driven by the potential for athletic scholarships, lucrative salaries, commercial endorsements, or some combination of all three, talented young athletes and their supporters have different motivations and expectations today than in the past. Participation in sport is now about much more than the experience itself or being physically fit or building character. For the few that aspire to be the best, it is about a grind that never stops – a continuous investment of time, money, and emotional energy in pursuit of an uncertain future with no guarantee of success.

In a compelling critical review of the influence of money on sport, Woelfel (2018, May) articulates that there is considerable concern in officiating circles about changing societal attitudes and the impact they have on organized sport. He posits that such attitudes have a negative impact on officials because they "...often manifest themselves in the belief, stated or otherwise, that a particular team or player is entitled to a desired outcome, whether it be the result of a particular game, attaining a college scholarship, or a similar tangible reward" (p. 62). This sense of entitlement is driven by the large time and financial investments (and in some cases long-term debt) sustained by parents in supporting their children to make it to the elite levels of competition. It also, according to the author, may contribute to "an environment where the principles of sportsmanship and ethical behaviour have been swept aside" (p. 62) and "...a new generation of parents who in many cases do not hold the student-athletes accountable..." for their actions (p. 63). Instead, helicopter parents (i.e., mothers and fathers who hover over their children) swoop down to pull them from harm's way, whether that threat is perceived or real. Every parent wants their child to enjoy success in everything that they do. In sport, success is all too often solely equated with winning. However, sport by its very nature is competitive – it purposely places athletes within a codified environment that is destined to identify a single winner amongst many. The simple yet critical perspective that has been lost is that not everyone can win.

There is no simple answer or obvious solution to these changing societal attitudes or trends, but they need to be acknowledged and problematized if a solution is to be found. In the short term, we offer the following two points of advice. First, it is obvious that officiating today is very different than it was in the past and, as such, that the ways and means of helping officials to gain skills and build competencies have to change (Mano, 2019, February). Simply running officiating clinics in classrooms, asking individuals to memorize rule books, and providing only a few hours of technical training prior to tossing them into competition will be insufficient if we hope to successfully recruit, train, develop, and advance officials in a sustainable way. The training of the next generation of officials will require investments in sport-specific, deliberate practice and training regimes that address the unique physical, intellectual, and emotional needs of each sport official. This will include a reliance on existing technologies (e.g., web-based course delivery) to overcome geography as a barrier and to distribute expert instruction at a distance, as well as the use of emerging technologies (e.g., augmented and virtual reality, or point of view and 360-degree camera recordings), to immerse officials in actual and simulated competitive situations as appropriate.

Second, historically, sports officials have been convenient scapegoats and targets of spectators' wrath when the outcome of a contest is less than desirable, often contributing to cynicism toward officials and rules of modern sport. Indeed, from an officiating perspective, there is a common notion that officials should find ways to depersonalize abusive interactions from spectators and other sport participants. This provides one example of a repositioned and displaced ownership of the problem. However, in an ideal world, everyone in sport (i.e., athletes, coaches, spectators, and officials) needs to start reframing and normalizing various aspects of their sport experience. This includes taking responsibility for one's actions, positive or negative, and the role that those actions play in determining the outcome of any competition. In as much as cell phone videos shared via social media have exposed officials to heightened levels of criticism, the same technologies may also prove useful in holding athletes, coaches, and spectators to a higher level of accountability than ever before.

Technology and Officiating Decision-making

The name Ken Pagan may not mean much to you, but the 2016 incident involving a beer can hurled from the stands and almost hitting a Baltimore Orioles outfielder during the seventh inning of an American League baseball game against the Toronto Blue Jays may stir memories of the social media firestorm that followed. YouTube and Twitter lit up with videos and images in an attempt to identify the offender, and within days, the man at the center of an incident that embarrassed the Blue Jays organization, the City of Toronto, and Canadians in general walked away from his job in news media. Yet Pagan's story is not unique. Photos and videos highlighting distasteful behavior or interference from fans at professional and grassroots sporting events emerge daily on mainstream news and social media platforms. Understanding the power of such platforms, media consultant Brian Barlow from Broken Arrow, Oklahoma, authors a popular Facebook page entitled "Offside" to post videos of individuals – athletes, coaches, and spectators – acting poorly toward officials and especially young officials (Tietz, 2019, April). Built around the acronym STOP – *Stop Tormenting Officials Permanently* – Barlow's motivations stemmed from threats from parents directed toward his 12-year-old daughter after officiating a soccer match between 6-year-olds. To Barlow, using video to hold those who abuse officials accountable is no different from using video to hold officials accountable. Although he has received some opposition to his efforts which have been interpreted by some as a public shaming experiment, he also posts and encourages contributions from others of videos displaying positive behaviors and selfies of officials posing with teams or with individual players. Whether you like the approach or not, the STOP initiative provides a rather salient example of how technology – digital photos and videos combined with social media platforms – is fueling a lower level of tolerance in sport for poor officiating and to a lesser degree, unacceptable participant and spectator behavior.

Technology is omnipresent around the world and within sport in the 21st century, yet it is unlikely that the average individual has a fulsome idea how pervasive it is currently or how large a role it will play in the future of sport and sport officiating. Technological innovations are part of how we experience sport and have been since the introduction of video replay for the purposes of reviewing (and potentially changing) the calls of officials. It began with the introduction of televised video replays in the sport of professional football – first by the now defunct United States Football League in 1984 and shortly thereafter by the National Football League in 1985 – and the simple notion that video technology could be an effective tool for improving the accuracy of the officiating task. However, what began with the use of single or perhaps dual camera angles and slow motion replays has evolved at a rapid rate to today support elaborate decision-making processes involving multifaceted technological platforms. The use of close up images, multiple camera angles, and ultra high speed slow motion frame-by-frame replays now aid and reinforce secondary appraisals of officials' decisions. These reviews, and the judgments they yield, also often extend beyond the site of the competition to include replay analysts at a distance. In professional sport, they also lead to athletes, coaches, and spectators turning their attention to large screen slow motion replays the instant that they perceive that a questionable call has occurred. Admittedly, these reviews do on occasion lead to different outcomes, either because of additional pictorial evidence afforded by a given camera angle not within the sightline of the official or by ultra-slow motion images which are not perceptible to the human eye. To this end some suggest and advocate for the use of technology as a quality control mechanism given the social and economic importance of sports today (Royce, 2012), and argue that its use as an aid to officiating judgments is therefore justifiable (Bordner, 2015). However, it is equally important to acknowledge that not all video replay reviews lead to overturned controversy-free calls. There is also emerging evidence that referees penalize situations more severely in slow motion compared to real time, which may have an important impact on the disciplinary decisions that result (Spitz, Moors, Wagemans, & Helsen, 2018). Critics also point out that the technology is expensive, and that it has led to a loss of the human element in sport, the marginalization of officials, and an attitude among spectators that all wrong decision-making in sport is unacceptable (Johnson & Taylor, 2016). Acknowledging these shortcomings is important; however, these alone should not dissuade us from the use of technology in less obtrusive ways to assist in officiating decisions.

At every level in sport, success or failure is determined by fractional differences in performance measured via time- or position-related data. To this end, relatively recent (i.e., post 2000) innovations in technology (e.g., starting block detection systems) promise to all but eliminate the potential for inaccurate decision-making with respect to certain types of sport performance infractions (e.g., false starts in competitive swimming or 100 m sprint track races). There is also obvious value in linking the shrill sound of a referee's whistle to stop the game clock during a basketball match, thereby ensuring that valuable seconds are not lost in a situation where a timekeeper may be unable to hear and quickly respond to the sound of the whistle in a noisy environment. Similarly, the electronic hogline in the sport of curling detects when a curler violates the rules by failing to release the handle of the curling rock before crossing the hogline boundary. When technological innovations such as these are unobtrusive in nature and of known reliability, have clarity of purpose, and contribute to a fair and equitable competition environment, they stand to gain wide acceptance within sporting circles.

Computer-based visualization systems (e.g., Hawk-Eye^{TM}) and Video Assistant Referee (VAR) technologies hold similar promise, and especially so as the resolution and hence accuracy of such devices improve. Using multiple high-performance cameras, computer-based visualization (CBV) systems are best known for their ability to combine projectile trajectory and speed data to create three-dimensional representations of the predicted flight path of a ball or puck and where it will interact with playing area features (e.g., boundary lines, goal posts, the strike zone in baseball, or the undulations of a golf green). In the sport of taekwondo, and applied in a different way to monitor competitor behavior, this technology has shown to be useful in reducing illegal play and tactics (Leveaux & Soliman, 2009). As a result, computer-based visualization systems have increasingly gained acceptance for use at the elite levels of numerous sports around the world (e.g., tennis, cricket, hurling, and soccer) as a secondary and objective means of adjudication via replay review. Although high-profile athletes like tennis' Roger Federer have on occasion been correct in challenging the fallibility of such systems, most sport observers do not realize the imprecision of such machines, appearing instead to favor a world where everything can be objectified through measurement and calibration (Hsu, 2017). Similarly, VAR technology has now gained strong acceptance in elite soccer circles, providing the opportunity for officials to review significant game situations and crucial officiating decisions associated with them, if required. With the use of slow motion and computer-enhanced images captured at multiple angles, the VAR can improve the accuracy of in-game decisions.

The world of sport has gradually come to accept the use of CBV and VAR technologies over time, yet it is important to note that these highly visible high-tech systems also have their critics and the criticisms come from multiple perspectives. For example, there is mounting evidence that the financial investment required to use such systems versus the actual decision accuracy gained (i.e., measured in terms of the number of officiating decisions that are actually changed as a result of review) is significant. Borooah (2016), for example, estimates that the use of Hawk-Eye^{TM} technology in cricket equates to operational costs of about US\$100,000 per match. He further argues that the same gains (i.e., the relatively few changes in decisions made as a result of reviews in any given match) may also possibly be obtained by investing the same money into long-term official education and training rather than technology. Second, and in a similar vein, while the use of the VAR does occasionally lead to a change of in-game officiating decisions, it has gained a mixed reception from players, coaches, and the public with regard to its utility as well as the observation that it interrupts the fluidity of the game. Officiating advocates, moreover, argue that the VAR may increase officials' anxiety and stress levels, and especially so in cases where they feel that their authority is being undermined. As sports look to improve the application of game laws with the use of CBV and AVR technologies, they should at the same time be concerned with enhancing the image of their officials. There are others, however, who argue that the human element should be entirely removed from officiating, arguing instead that with technology – including the use of machine learning and artificial intelligence systems – human officials may no longer be required.

Dr. Ian Pearson, a leading futurologist, is predicting that the refereeing of elite soccer matches by robots will occur as soon as the year 2030 (Livesey, 2018). This may seem like somewhat of a far-flung idea, however, so too did self-driving cars not that long ago. Without going into too much detail, the notion is that by integrating large amounts of real-time data generated from many different sources (e.g., computerized visualization systems; nanosensors embedded within the clothing worn by athletes, game implements, and projected objects), athletic performances may be effectively monitored without human intervention. This includes being able to predict and call penalizing behaviors (e.g., potentially injurious collisions or obstructions) in invasion games (e.g., soccer, ice hockey, lacrosse) or in environments where athletes share a common competition space (e.g., squash) by knowing the position of each individual, the rate at which they are moving and turning, and who occupied the space initially. Like it or not, it is predicted that these technologies will reduce the need for human involvement in officiating, thereby reducing judgment errors and leading to more accurate decisions (Ghafourifar, 2017). Only time will tell if Pearson's prediction of robot referees in elite soccer will come to fruition, yet we must admit that technology is pervasive in sport as we know it, whether it is classified as being "low-tech" (e.g., hand-held stopwatches) or "high-tech" (e.g., computerized visualization systems) in nature.

The question that remains is whether the human official can be replaced in totality? In sports like ice hockey, where certain rules (e.g., high sticking) may lead to differing penalties depending on intent, it's not clear how machine-generated data can fully assess an action underpinned by emotions like anger and frustration. Equally important to emphasize, however, is that in as much as technology may be affordable and of value at the elite levels of competition, human decision-making will *always* have a role to play in officiating sport. This is especially true at the youth and amateur sport levels where it will be too costly to implement high-tech systems in the most rudimentary of venues, and especially so in those located within small, rural, or isolated communities. Grassroots officiating education and mentoring programs are a necessity and will continue to be critical in supporting youth and amateur sport as we know it. It is from this large talent pool moreover that the next generation of elite officials will evolve to ply their trade, with or without the assistance of technology. Ensuring that the talent pool is constantly growing in size, by improving both the image of officiating as an avocation and the implementation of effective recruitment strategies, and by retaining those who have already entered into the system, will be essential if we want to develop highly skilled and competent officials. Growing the talent pool will also require the world of sport to open its doors and to be welcoming and supportive to all who want to excel as officials within it.

Equity, Diversity, and Inclusion

In the complex domain of organized sport where the privilege to participate has historically been the exclusive domain of able-bodied males, discussions of equity, diversity, and inclusion are necessary. Defined in the simplest of forms, equity is about ensuring that everyone has an equal opportunity to participate while diversity is about recognizing differences between people and groups of people and placing values on those differences. Inclusion, in contrast, refers to the creation of environments in which participation by any individual or group is welcomed, respected, supported, and valued. While institutionalized sport still has a long way to go in this regard (Fink, 2016), rising participation by previously marginalized or absent groups provides evidence that real progress has been made in creating more equitable opportunities for athletic participation. There are a number of reasons for this, not the least of which includes the 20th-century women's movement which led to the introduction of women in sport policies and to a lesser extent legislation (e.g., Title IX in the United States) to enhance female participation in sport. High-profile litigation cases demanding equal pay for men and women in elite sport (e.g., 2019 U.S. Women's Soccer team members versus U.S. Soccer) provide evidence that the fight for gender equality in sport has been active and remained active over a 50-year period. Moreover, the pioneering efforts of Eunice Kennedy Schreiber in support of the Special Olympics movement and the growth of parasport on the world stage, including the Olympic Games, have opened the doors to the differently able. And today, Prince Harry's support for military veterans and the Invictus Games continues to broaden these boundaries as do government-led policies designed to enhance involvement in sport. The value of physical activity through sport in enhancing physical, cognitive, and emotional well-being is now well established within the scientific literature and to this end, sport should be a domain open to all.

With all of this said true equity in sport for females as athletes continues to be elusive, as too does involvement in sport-specific roles including officiating (Fink, 2016; Tingle, Warner, & Sartore-Baldwin, 2014). Numbers vary from country to country, yet national census figures aggregated across all amateur sports in Canada effectively illustrate this point with males outnumbering women by a ratio of 3:2 as athletes and to a greater extent by a ratio of 3:1 when it comes to officiating (Heritage Canada, 2013). For the sport of soccer in Canada, these numbers are mirrored with 41% of all registered soccer players and 23% of all soccer referees, respectfully, being female (Reid, 2016). On a world level more people participate in soccer than in any other sport, yet somewhat surprisingly, only 10% of all soccer officials globally are female (Reid, 2016). Moreover, in South Korea only 5.2% and in England only 3.6% of all soccer officials are female (Frampton, 2014; Kim & Hong, 2016). Although we have chosen soccer to illustrate this issue, it is important to acknowledge that disproportionate underrepresentation of females in officiating is relatively common place and not unique to this one sport. Furthermore, in some sports such as artistic swimming, the number of female officials may be considerably larger than the number of male officials. The question that remains, however, is why these gender imbalances occur and especially so, now that it is increasingly common for women to officiate men's matches and vice versa? This observation alone invalidates distinctions based on gender and the capacity for success in the role as a referee, umpire, or judge (Fink, 2016; Kim & Hong, 2016), as does the observation that females and males are equally resilient and motivated to enter into officiating.

In our study of 1,073 active Canadian amateur sport officials from over 37 different sports, both males and females exhibited high levels of resilience (or the ability to cope with adversity) and were seen to garner a high degree of satisfaction and enjoyment from their efforts (Livingston & Forbes, 2016). In fact, for young officials aged 20 years or less, young women demonstrated higher levels of motivation and excitement to be in the role than their male counterparts. However, as age increased, motivational levels for females systematically declined while those for males remained relatively stable. Given the purpose of our study, we were unable to infer causality for these trends, yet the findings of other investigations and reports of the lived experiences of females as officials offer interesting insights into potential contributing factors.

Schaeperkoetter's (2017) autoethnography paints a rather grim picture of an extremely motivated young woman – an accomplished athlete and a highly educated individual in her own right – facing multiple points of resistance based on her gender from fellow officials, players, coaches, parents, and game assignors in her early days of basketball officiating. She describes in detail how she was made to feel like an outsider and someone who constantly needed to prove herself to advance to officiating the next level of competition, while tolerating sexist remarks and reactions. The marginalization, lack of respect, and resulting stress that she experienced are common and consistent themes echoed in numerous critical examinations of the lived experiences of female officials within the sports of basketball (Tingle et al., 2014; Warner, Tingle, & Kellett, 2013), rugby (Baldwin & Vallance, 2016), soccer (Forbes, Edwards, & Fleming, 2015; Kim & Hong, 2016; Reid, 2016), and sport in general (Fink, 2016; Rauscher & Cooky, 2016). The issue of limited female participation in the sport officiating ranks does not in all cases appear to be primarily related to having an opportunity to enter into the system, but rather the failure of existing sport systems to value *and* support those females already present in the interest of retaining them. Therefore, this is not so much a problem of equity (i.e., having the opportunity to enter into the system) but rather one of diversity (i.e., the institutionalized culture of sport failing to value their presence) and inclusion (i.e., entry into environments which are less than welcoming, supportive, or respectful). And it is likely that these issues extend beyond the realm of gender when it comes to other marginalized groups interested in sport officiating.

In preparing to write this book, we could find no scientific articles examining sport officiating within the realm of parasport or discussion of parasport athletes themselves aspiring to officiating careers. We did, however, find and highlight in Chapter 1 of this book the inspiring story of Bailey Slusher, a teenaged basketball official from Indiana. What we did not mention – because it is an irrelevant point – was that Bailey performs his officiating duties while seated in a wheelchair. This leads us to question whether institutionalized sport as we know it either explicitly or implicitly privileges the able bodied over those who are not? In several countries around the world, including Canada, existing human right codes would not allow individuals with physical limitations or anomalies to be unreasonably excluded from the opportunity to officiate. Officiating purists may disagree with this point. However, while an individual born with polysyndactyly (i.e., congenital malformations of the fingers, including the presence of additional or webbed fingers) might experience challenges in using traditional hand signals to identify the awarding of two points or three points for a successful score in the sport of basketball, there is no substantive reason as to why an alternate method of communicating that result (e.g., a verbal signal) could not be utilized. In the absence of evidence to support these suppositions, it is difficult to add anything further on this topic. However, it does identify a major gap in the scientific literature, and to that end, it is an area that deserves and requires attention in future investigations of sport officiating.

Summary

There is much to be done if the marginalization of sport officials within institutionalized sport is to be adequately stemmed and eliminated in favor of promoting the avocation as a valued and important aspect of each and every competition from the grassroots to the elite levels. The three topics highlighted in this chapter were chosen because they each speak to a different issue which affects the participation of individuals as sport officials within sport as we know it today. For example, the professionalization of youth sport has slowly transformed sport from a pastime which was valued for the sake of participation and its physical and purported character building benefits – including the ability to get along and work with others in teams – to one that now emphasizes individual success for the sake of potential future monetary rewards and prestige. With athletes, coaches, and even parents aspiring to benefit from the athletic success of their children, any real or perceived challenge to that ultimate goal – including an officiating decision – is tested. As a result, officiating today is more physically, intellectually, and emotionally trying than it ever has been in the past. More recently, technology has added to these challenges by adding evidence in the form of video or audio data to the debate. However, of equal if not more import with respect to technology is the fact that we have no real idea of how technology may contribute to officiating in either a positive or negative sense tomorrow or into the future. It may also displace humans from certain officiating roles, but we would argue that there will always be a need for human decision-makers in sport. This need will be most acute at the grassroots and entry levels of sport where expensive, high-tech systems will not be affordable or even desirable, in sport. As such sport organizations and administrators will need to continue to actively recruit, develop, retain, and advance individuals to fill the roles of referee, umpire, and judge. Moreover, as governments continue to promote through policy more active involvement in sport by the masses, there will be a need for more individuals to become officials. To this end, sport must provide opportunities for those with an interest in the role to participate, value the diversity and differing perspectives they bring to the task, and create an environment that fosters a sense of belonging as well as a desire to remain.

Doing all of this will require significant cultural changes within sport as we know it today. It is never easy to change culture, or even sometimes to simply stand up and address a problem that exists, but it must be done. There is good reason to believe that this will happen and to say that the future is looking brighter for officials now that sport scientists, administrators, and organizations are beginning to value them by addressing with interest the challenges and opportunities associated with the role. The importance of including sport officials in the sport science agenda cannot be overlooked. To this end, we openly encourage and invite those with an interest in this field of study to actively engage in helping to answer the large number of questions that remain. After all, without officials sport merely becomes play.

TAKE AWAY MESSAGES FROM THIS CHAPTER

- Today's sport official – rightly or wrongly – faces new and immediate challenges to their authority in a world of sport with many changing and competing expectations and interests.
- How sport officials participate and perform their role in the future will inevitably be influenced by different issues pervasive to officials and all sport participants.

Professionalization of Youth Sport

- Athletic scholarships, lucrative salaries, and commercial endorsements drive talented young athletes to have different motivations and expectations.
- The ways and means of sports officials gathering skills and competencies have to change because organized sport has changed.

(Continued)

- The next generation of officials will require investments in sport-specific, deliberate practice and training to navigate challenges brought about by a more demanding performance environment and professionalized youth sport culture.

Officiating Decision-making and Inception of New Technologies

- Technology has the power to hold all participants (i.e., athletes, coaches, spectators, and officials) in sport accountable for their actions. Accountability for one's actions should not solely rest with those in the officiating role.
- When technological innovations are unobtrusive in nature and of known accuracy, have clarity of purpose, and contribute to a fair and equitable competition environment by improving officials' decision-making, they stand to gain wide acceptance within sporting circles.

Equity, Diversity, and Inclusion in Sport Officiating

- Discussions of equity, diversity, and inclusion are essential relative to participation in sport and specific roles within it, including officiating.
- Female participation rates in sport lag behind those of their male counterparts, with participation rates being more disparate in the officiating as compared to the playing ranks.
- Considering that it is now common at the elite level in sports such as soccer and rugby for women to officiate men's matches and vice versa, distinctions based on gender and the capacity for success in the role are no longer valid.
- Females and males are equally resilient and motivated to enter into officiating.
- The issue of limited female participation in the sport officiating ranks does not appear to be one of having an opportunity to enter into the system, but rather the failure of existing sport systems to value *and* support the presence of females in the interest of retaining them.
- There is an absolute dearth of scientific studies examining sport officiating within the realm of parasport, or discussion of parasport athletes themselves aspiring to officiating careers.
- Sport must provide opportunities for those with an interest in officiating to participate, value the diversity and differing perspectives they bring to the task, and create an environment that fosters a sense of belonging as well as a desire to remain.

References

Baldwin, C.F., & Vallance, R. (2016). Women referees experiences officiating Rugby Union. *Women in Sport and Physical Activity Journal, 24*, 152–161. doi:10.1123/wspaj.2015-0036

Bordner, S.S. (2015). Call 'em as they are: What's wrong with blown calls and what to do about them. *Journal of the Philosophy of Sport, 42*, 101–120. doi: 10.1080/00948705.2014.911096

Borooah, V.K. (2016). Upstairs and downstairs: The imperfections of cricket's decision review system. *Journal of Sports Economics, 17*(1), 64–85.

Brower, J. (1979). The professionalization of organized youth sport: Social psychological impacts and outcomes. *Annals of the American Academy of Political and Social Science, 445*, 39–46.

Fink, J.S. (2016). Hidden in plain sight: The embedded nature of sexism in sport. *Journal of Sport Management, 30*, 1–7.

Forbes, A., Edwards, L., & Fleming, S. (2015). "Women can't referee": Exploring the experiences of female football officials within UK football culture. *Soccer & Society, 16*, 521–539. doi:10.1080/14660970.2014.882829

Frampton, J. (2014). Official's call. In C. MacMahon, D. Mascarenhas, H. Plessner, A. Pizzera, R. Oudejans, & M. Raab (Eds.), *Sports officials and officiating: Science and practice* (pp. 24–30). London: Routledge.

Ghafourifar, A. (2017, February 4). What would the super bowl look like with AI referees? *Entefy.* Retrieved April 19, 2019 from https://venturebeat.com/2017/02/04/what-would-the-super-bowl-look-like-with-ai-referees/

Heritage Canada. (2013). *Sport participation 2010: Research paper.* Ottawa: Government of Canada.

Hsu, H. (2017, March 30). What if we had perfect robot referees? *The New Yorker.* Retrieved April 19, 2019 from http://www.newyorker.com/culture/cultural-comment/what-if-we-had-perfect-robot-referees

Johnson, C., & Taylor, J. (2016). Rejecting technology: A normative defense of fallible officiating. *Sport, Ethics and Philosophy, 10*, 148–160. doi:10.1080/17511321.2016.1152287

Kim, M., & Hong, E. (2016). A red card for women: Female officials ostracized in South Korean football. *Asian Journal of Women's Studies, 22*, 114–130.

Leveaux, R., & Soliman, K.S. (2009, November 9–10). Using technology in sport to support referee's decision making. *Proceedings of the 13th International Business Information Management Association Conference* (pp. 1184–1191). Marrakech, Morocco.

Livesey, J. (2018, February 15). Robot football referees and linesmen could be reality by 2030 with humanoid PLAYERS not far behind. *The Mirror.* Retrieved April 19, 2019 from http://www.mirror.co.uk/sport/football/news/robot-football-referees-linesmen-could-12030671

Livingston, L.A., & Forbes, S.L. (2016). Factors contributing to the retention of Canadian amateur sport officials: Motivations, perceived organizational support, and resilience. *International Journal of Sports Science & Coaching, 11*, 342–355.

Mano, B. (2019, February). See that "train" A coming. *Referee, 44*(2), 4.

Rauscher, L., & Cooky, C. (2016). Ready for anything the world gives her? A critical look at sports-based positive youth development for girls. *Sex Roles, 74*, 288–298.

Reid, K. (2016). *The untold stories of women soccer referees*. Unpublished Master's thesis, University of Ottawa, Ottawa, ON, Canada.

Royce, R. (2012). Refereeing and technology – reflections of Collins' proposals. *Journal of the Philosophy of Sport, 39,* 53–64. doi:10.1080/00948705.2012. 675066

Schaeperkoetter, C.C. (2017). Basketball officiating as a gendered arena: An autoethnography. *Sport Management Review, 20,* 128–141.

Spitz, J., Moors, P., Wagemans, J., & Helsen, W.F. (2018). The impact of video speed on the decision-making process of sports officials. *Cognitive Research – Principles and Implications, 3.* doi:10.1186/s41235-018-0105-8

Tietz, S. (2019, April). STOP! Stop Tormenting officials permanently. Referee tackles bad behavior. *Referee, 44*(4), 50–55.

Tingle, J.K., Warner, S., & Sartore-Baldwin, M.L. (2014). The experience of former women officials and the impact on the sporting environment. *Sex Roles, 71,* 7–20.

Warner, S., Tingle, J.K., & Kellett, P. (2013). Officiating attrition: The experiences of former referees via a sport development lens. *Journal of Sport Management, 27,* 316–328.

Woelfel, R. (2018, May). Money ball. *Referee, 43*(5), 58–63.

Index